Celebrate
Holi
With Me!

From The Toddler Diaries

Written by Shoumi Sen
Illustrated by Abira Das

To Dida & Thakuma...for all the stories

There's joy in every step
As the birds start to sing,
As we bid winter goodbye
And get ready for Spring!

If we haven't met before,
Let's get introduced already
I'm Riya, what's your name?
Will you play Holi with me?

We celebrate Holi
At the beginning of Spring,
This is the Festival of Colors
Oh, the joy that it will bring!

He wanted all to worship him,
Of his son he asked the same
But all the boy, Prahlad, would utter
Was Lord Vishnu's name!

The angry king tried many ways
To hurt Prahlad, but failed,
Snakes and elephants could do no harm
For the child's devotion prevailed.

In despair, the king now turned
To Holika, his evil sis,
"Destroy him!" he cried,
"So my life will be full of bliss"

Holika hatched an evil plan
As she could not be hurt by fire,
She took Prahlad in her lap
And climbed onto a burning pyre.

Prahlad was calm as ever
To Lord Vishnu he prayed,
Holika was destroyed instead
And the little boy was saved!

As we celebrate Holi
Let's remember this trend
That evil, like Holika, burns
And good prevails in the end!

Dol Jatra, Phagwah or Fagu
Call Holi what you may,
Old or young, boy or girl
All together we will play!

The pile of logs is growing
There's excitement in the air,
Pyramids of abeer and gulal
There's color everywhere!

The bonfire is lit on Choti Holi
We'll play Holi tomorrow,
We call this Holika Dahan
The destruction of evil and sorrow.

We meet at our favorite corner
It's finally Holi today,
And we march through our neighborhood
With shouts of "Holi Hai!"

I spray my friend with my pichkari,
And smear abeer on his face,
We throw balloons on each other
And many others join the chase.

My friends have buckets of water
And they empty them on my head
I'm a rainbow of colors
Blue, yellow, pink and red!

But Holi isn't for kids alone
Even our parents join the fray,
Spare no one from color
Is the motto of the day!

Without music and dance,
Holi isn't complete
As we all let our hair down
And dance to the dholak's beat!

Soon we can't recognize each other
And my Ma says with a smile
"Look at you, my Riya,
Clean up today will take a while!"

The best part is yet to come,
Yummy food and sweets await;
Gujiya, mathri and malpoa
Make their way on to my plate!

We meet our friends in the evening
And remember the fun we had today,
We're making plans already,
For next Holi, a year away!

Toddler Dictionary

Abeer Made of natural or synthetic materials, Abeer is what gives the colored powders of Holi their shine. Shiny crystals of Abeer are mixed with Gulaal (colored powder) and this combination is what people use to play Holi.

Bollywood Name given to the Hindi film industry based in Mumbai (formerly known as Bombay), Bombay+Hollywood led to the name Bollywood.

Choti Holi On this first day of Holi, a bonfire is lit, signifying the destruction of Prahlad's evil aunt, Holika. The bonfire signifies the victory of good over evil.

Dholak A two-headed hand drum popular in Northern India.

Dol Jatra Holi is celebrated as Dol Jatra in the Indian state of West Bengal.

Fagu Another name for Holi; Holi is celebrated as Fagu in Nepal.

Gujiya A deep fried pastry with a sweet filling that is often served during Holi.

Gulal Colored powder that is mixed with Abeer and used to celebrate Holi.

Holi This 'Festival of Colors' celebrates the victory of good over evil. People celebrate by throwing colors on each other and spraying each other with colored water. It is a joyful occasion, accompanied by music and dancing.

Holi Hai Joyful shouts of Holi Hai! (It's Holi!) can be heard as people celebrating Holi smear each other with colored powder or water.

Holika Dahan A bonfire is lit on Choti Holi and this practice is called Holika Dahan. It signifies the destruction of Holika and the victory of good over evil.

Malpoa A delicious Indian dessert that looks like a pancake.

Mathri A crispy, flavorful Indian snack made of flour.

Phagwah Another name for Holi.

Pichkari A colorful water gun that is used to spray water on others during Holi.

About the Author

'From The Toddler Diaries' started as a series of poems that Shoumi wrote for her daughter. This collection, in its stapled makeshift binding, was the center of several bedtime story sessions and play dates with friends. Inspired by this interest amongst kids and encouraged by their parents, she decided to publish the collection.

Shoumi is a Strategy, Sales and Marketing professional at a leading Energy Management company. She grew up in Mumbai and Dubai and studied Engineering at BITS Pilani and the University of Maryland. She loves to travel, has lived and worked in many countries, and currently lives in Los Angeles, California with her husband and daughter.

Visit Shoumi's website: www.shoumisen.com
Facebook: https://www.facebook.com/FromTheToddlerDiaries

About the Illustrator

From a very early age Abira was interested in the magical world of illustration and cartoons. She completed her graduation in Multimedia, Animation and Illustration from St. Xavier's College, Kolkata. She has worked on many books for authors from different countries and her illustrated books are available on Amazon.com.

Connect with Abira: www.abira-darkhues.blogspot.com

Also in the series 'From The Toddler Diaries'

Celebrate Durga Puja With Me!

UNIT 2

LIFE IN THE UNITED STATES

People walk around Times Square, New York City.

CIVICS Learn about the average American; read about community colleges in the United States

ACADEMIC Take a survey; read and understand infographics; represent information in graphs and charts

AT WORK Read about income taxes

On July 4, Americans celebrate their independence with parades, concerts, and fireworks.

A **CIVICS** Read about the average American. Guess and circle the information.

1. The average American lives in **a house / an apartment / a condo**.
2. The typical American family has **one child / two children / three children.**
3. About a third of people eat breakfast **at home / at work / on the go**.
4. The average person drinks **one / two / three** cup(s) of coffee a day.
5. Most Americans **take a bus / walk / drive** to work.
6. The average American consumes **5 / 50 / over 150** pounds of sugar in one year.
7. The average family has **one / two / three** TV(s).
8. Most Americans check their phones **30 / 50 / 80** times a day.
9. The average American changes jobs every **four / seven / ten** years.
10. The average person moves **five / eight / eleven** times in his or her lifetime.

1. a house 2. two children 3. on the go 4. two 5. drive 6. over 150 7. two 8. 80 9. four 10. eleven

B Circle or complete the statements about your life. Then, read your sentences to a partner.

1. I live in **a house / an apartment / a condo**.

2. My family has **one / two / three /** _____ child / children.

3. I eat breakfast **at home / at work / on the go**.

4. I **take a bus / walk / drive /** _____ to work.

5. I eat **one / two / three /** _____ hamburger(s) a week.

6. My family has **one / two / three /** _____ TV(s).

7. I check my phone **30 / 50 / 80 /** _____ times a day.

C Listen and complete the chart. Then, compare Charlie to the average American male. 🎧6

Charlie	The Average American Male
32 – single	gets married at 27
is _____ _____ tall	is 5'10" tall
weighs _____ pounds	weighs 195 pounds
likes / doesn't like his job	likes his job
works _____ hours a day	works eight hours a day
earns $_____ a year	earns $43,056 a year
lives in a / an _____	lives in a house
_____ to work	drives to work
has / doesn't have a pet	has a pet

> The average American male gets married at 27. Charlie is 32, and he is single.

ACTIVE GRAMMAR — Simple Present

Affirmative Statements	
I You We They	work. eat breakfast.
He She It	work**s**. eat**s** breakfast.

Negative Statements		
I You We They	**don't**	work. eat breakfast.
He She It	**doesn't**	work. eat breakfast.

The simple present describes routines and activities that happen every day, every week, every month, and so on.

A **AT WORK** Complete with the correct form of the verb. Some of the verbs are negative.

1. April 15th (or around that date) is tax day in the United States. People (need) _____*need*_____ to file their income taxes by that date.

2. Most states also (have) _____ a state income tax, but a few states (have) _____ any state income tax.

3. If a person (make) _____ a high income, that person usually (pay) _____ more taxes.

4. Some people (owe) _____ a lot in taxes, but some people (owe) _____ anything. For example, if a person's income is under $10,000, she (pay) _____ anything.

5. If a person (overpay) _____ his taxes, the government (send) _____ him a refund. More than 80% of all taxpayers (receive) _____ a refund.

B Interview a classmate. How are your days similar? How are they different?

	You	Your Partner
1. Do you eat breakfast every day?		
2. Do you work full time?		
3. Do you take public transportation to school?		
4. Do you use a computer every day?		
5. Do you cook for your family?		
6. Do you have classes every day?		
7. Do you go to bed before midnight?		

Yes, I do.
No, I don't.

C **Pronunciation: Final -s** Listen and repeat. 🎧**7**

/s/	/z/	/iz/
likes	owns	watches
wants	drives	uses
takes	studies	dances

D Circle the sound you hear. 🎧**8**

1. /s/ (/z/) /iz/
2. /s/ /z/ /iz/
3. /s/ /z/ /iz/

4. /s/ /z/ /iz/
5. /s/ /z/ /iz/
6. /s/ /z/ /iz/

7. /s/ /z/ /iz/
8. /s/ /z/ /iz/
9. /s/ /z/ /iz/

E **STUDENT TO STUDENT**

Student 1: Turn to Appendix C. Read the sentences in Set A.

Student 2: Look at the picture. Listen and write the sentences under *Josh* or *Sam*.

Then, change roles. Student 2, turn to Appendix C and read the sentences in Set B. Student 1, write the sentences under *Josh* or *Sam*.

Josh	Sam
1. _____	1. _____
2. _____	2. _____
3. _____	3. _____

Singular Subject	
The average person	
The average man	**has** a cellphone.
The average woman	**drives** to work.
The man	**works** full time.
The woman	

Plural Subject	
Most Americans	**have** a cellphone.
Most people	**drive** to work.
Fifty percent of people	**work** full time.

A Complete the sentences. Use the correct form of the verb.

1. The average adult (exercise) _____exercises_____ twenty minutes a day.

2. Most full-time workers (receive) _____ a paid vacation.

3. The average teenager (take) _____ a summer class.

4. Most Americans (drive) _____ to work.

5. The average person (sleep) _____ 6.5 hours a night.

6. Women (do) _____ 70 percent of the housework in a family.

7. The average person (use) _____ a computer every day.

B Listen and write the sentences that you hear. Your teacher will turn to Appendix D.

WORD PARTNERSHIPS	
50 percent	
half	of the students
about half	of the men
more than half	of the women
fewer than half	

Do you wear a seat belt?

90%
Wear a seat belt

10%
No seat belt

1. _____

2. _____

Do you rent or own your home?

36% Rent
64% Own their homes

3. _____

4. _____

5. _____

C ACADEMIC LET'S TALK. Work with a partner. Write sentences about each chart.

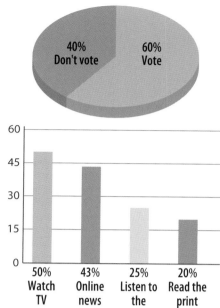

1. What percentage of Americans vote in national elections?

   a. _____

   _____

   b. _____

   _____

60

45

30

15

0

| 50% Watch TV | 43% Online news | 25% Listen to the radio | 20% Read the print newspaper |

2. How do most Americans get their news?

   a. _____

   _____

   b. _____

   _____

**67%
No
bachelor's
degree**

**33%
Bachelor's
degree**

3. Do most Americans have a bachelor's degree?

   a. _____

   _____

   b. _____

   _____

**77%
Drive to work**

 **10%
Carpool**

4. How do most Americans get to work?

   a. _____

   _____

   b. _____

 **5%
Public transportation**

 **4%
Work from home**

   _____

   c. _____

 **2.5%
Walk**

   _____

   d. _____

 **1.5%
Other**

   _____

ACTIVE GRAMMAR — Time Expressions

every morning	once a week	on the weekend	in the summer
every day	twice a month	on Sundays	in the winter
every night	three times a year		

Time expressions are usually placed at the end of a sentence.

A Complete the sentences about yourself. Use time expressions.

1. I study English _____.

2. I go to work _____.

3. I work overtime _____.

4. I go to the dentist _____.

5. I take a vacation _____.

6. I sleep late _____.

7. I buy new clothes _____.

8. I pay my bills _____.

9. I get a haircut _____.

10. I check my phone _____.

B Talk with a partner. How often do you do each activity listed?

> I go dancing every weekend.

> I go dancing once a year!

1. go dancing
2. eat out
3. call my family abroad
4. order a pizza
5. do the laundry
6. eat at a fast-food restaurant
7. exercise
8. go to a party
9. text my friends
10. check my email
11. go to the beach
12. watch TV

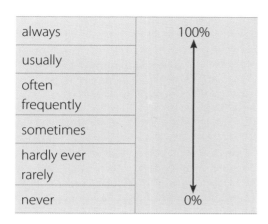

always	100%
usually	
often frequently	
sometimes	
hardly ever rarely	
never	0%

Put adverbs of frequency before most verbs.
I **often** walk in the park.
He **never** takes a taxi.
Put adverbs of frequency after the verb *be*.
I am **never** late for work.
She is **rarely** sick.

A Put the words in the correct order.

1. always / homework / do / I / my _____

2. tired / in the morning / He / always / is _____

3. her / She / rarely / sister / calls _____

4. class / is / interesting / usually / This _____

5. drives / He / always / too fast _____

6. weather / is / Florida / usually / in / The / beautiful _____

7. wear / They / their / always / seat belts _____

B Talk about yourself. Use an adverb of frequency in each sentence. Add two sentences of your own.

I always eat breakfast.

I never eat breakfast. I'm not hungry in the morning.

1. I eat breakfast.
2. I am polite.
3. I am homesick.
4. I get headaches.
5. I think about my future.

6. I am worried.
7. I go to bed early.
8. I do my homework.
9. I am late for class.
10. I take a taxi.

11. I am busy.
12. I lose my keys.
13. _____
14. _____

/ An American Family

A Listen. Under the pictures, write the missing information about the Shaw family. 🎧9

1.

Mr. Shaw: Hours: _____   Salary: _____

Mrs. Shaw: Hours: _____   Salary: _____

2.

Mr. Shaw: _____ minutes

Mrs. Shaw: _____ minutes

3.

$_____

4.

5.

6.

B Read about the average American family. Then, compare with the Shaw family.

1. Most husbands earn more than their wives.
   <u>Mrs. Shaw earns more than Mr. Shaw.</u>

2. Most workers drive to work.

3. The average family has one pet.

4. The average household is a mother and father and two children.

5. The average family takes a vacation twice a year.

6. Most families have two TVs.

C Complete with the correct form of the verb. Some of the verbs are negative.

1. Mr. Shaw (drive) _____<u>doesn't drive</u>_____ a minivan.

2. Mr. Shaw (work) _____ close to home.

3. Mrs. Shaw (take) _____ public transportation to work.

4. Mr. and Mrs. Shaw (have) _____ one child.

5. Mr. and Mrs. Shaw (live) _____ in an apartment.

6. Andy's parents (work) _____ part time.

7. Mrs. Shaw (work) _____ at a college.

8. The family (eat) _____ out once a week.

9. Andy (have) _____ a pet bird.

10. The Shaws and the grandparents (live) _____ in the same house.

> The word **family** is singular, but people often use **they** to talk about family.
> The **family** eats out on Friday night.
> **They** like Chinese or Italian food.

The Average Community College Student

About 40 percent of all college students in the United States attend community colleges. Community colleges are schools that offer two-year associate degrees and certificates and licenses in a large number of careers, such as paralegal, office assistant, and information technician. The 1,103 community colleges in the United States also **train** students for new jobs and offer courses in many subjects, including English as a second language.

Most community colleges have open admissions; they **accept** almost all students who apply. Thirty-six percent of the students are the first ones in their families to attend college. Most students need one or more **basic skills** courses in reading, writing, or math to prepare them for college-level classes. Sixty-two percent of full-time students work, so full-time schedules are difficult. More than 60 percent of all students attend school part time. The tuition at a community college is more **affordable** than at a four-year school. The average tuition is $3,570 a year, and more than half of the students receive some financial aid. Many of the students who begin at a community college **transfer** to a four-year college for their junior and senior years.

Emily is a typical community college student. She attends school part time. As a young woman, she is part of the 56 percent of all community college students who are women. She is 28 years old, the average age of a community college student. Emily's parents and her older brother graduated from high school, but she is the first person in her family to begin college.

Emily works full time in the admissions office in the county hospital. Her **goal** is to become a registered nurse. She is taking pre-nursing courses and has been accepted to the nursing program. Many of the nurses in the United States receive their degrees from community colleges.

Emily is a second-semester student. During her first semester, she needed to take a course in basic math. This semester, she is taking three courses. In the fall, Emily will attend school full time and work on the weekends. She applied for financial aid and is going to receive $1,500 a semester next year.

Most students take three years or more to **complete** their degrees at a community college. Emily hopes to have her nursing degree by the time she is 31. 🎧 10

Pasadena City College, in Pasadena, California, offers 114 associate degree programs and serves over 29,000 students.

A Discuss these questions.

1. Where do you study—at a community college, an adult school, a high school, or another kind of school?

2. What community college is nearest to your home? What programs does it offer?

B Circle the correct word or phrase.

1. The program will train him to be a (police officer) / **student**.

2. The school **accepts** many **students / classes** each semester.

3. The student needed a **basic skills** course in **reading / financial aid**.

4. The tuition at an **affordable** school is **reasonable / expensive**.

5. Some students transfer from a two-year college to a **four-year college / job**.

6. Emily's goal is to **become a nurse / apply to college**.

> **READING NOTE**
>
> **Finding Examples**
> A reading often gives facts about a topic. Then, it tells a story to give specific examples.

C **CIVICS** Read the facts about community college students. Find examples in the reading to show that Emily is a typical community college student.

1. Community college students are often the first ones in their families to attend college.
   Emily's parents and brother didn't go to college.
   _____

2. Most students need one or more basic skills courses.
   _____
   _____

3. Most students work full or part time.
   _____
   _____

4. More women than men attend community college.
   _____
   _____

5. More than half of the students receive some financial aid.
   _____
   _____

C **▶ WATCH** Watch the video about diversity in Queens, New York. How does this compare to diversity in your school?

A Read.

People enjoy a beach day in Rio de Janeiro, Brazil.

1 My family is from Brazil. Brazil is the largest country in South America and one of the largest countries in the world. The people of Brazil speak Portuguese.

2 Brazilians are outgoing, expressive people. When we meet, we kiss each other on both cheeks. Men pat one another on the back or give each other a hug. When we speak with a friend, we often touch or hold hands.

3 Families are the center and heart of our lives. Families usually live in the same city or in the same area of the city. Often, many members of a family live on the same block! We see each other almost every day. On the weekends, the younger cousins go out in groups together. There are few childcare centers because aunts and uncles and grandparents help care for the babies and younger children.

4 The main meal is lunch, in the early afternoon, between 12 and 2 p.m. We eat a lot of rice and beans and we know how to cook them many different ways. Lunch also includes meat or fish and a vegetable or a salad. On Sundays, the whole family often eats together. There is a lot of talking, laughing, and enjoying each other's company.

5 We enjoy sports, especially volleyball, basketball, and tennis. But the most popular sport is *futebol* (*soccer* in the United States). We think that our teams and players are the best in the world. Brazil has won the World Cup five times.

6 One of our favorite activities is going to the beach. The beaches are free. We put down our blankets, take out our suntan lotion, and turn on our stereos—loud! People walk along the beach selling food, drinks, hats, jewelry, and many other things. As the day continues, we begin to dance and it becomes like a party on the beach. We stay at the beach until late at night. Brazilians enjoy celebrations and parties. When you visit our country and receive your first invitation to a party, remember to come at least an hour late. In Brazil, we are very relaxed about time.

Adding Details

In a composition, each paragraph has one topic or idea. To make a story more interesting, include many details and examples about the topic.

B Write the topic of each paragraph in the reading.

1. _____ introduction _____

2. _____

3. _____

4. _____

5. _____

6. _____

C **LET'S TALK.** In groups, talk about the lives of average people in your country. Take notes. Some topics you can discuss are:

greetings	education
families	holidays
sports	weekend activities
food	religion
transportation	work

> In my country, most young people like to go to the beach when they are on vacation.

D Write a composition about the lives of average people in the country you are from. Choose three or four topics to write about. Give many details and examples. Use your notes from Exercise C.

E **CIVICS** Correct the mistake with the underlined verb. If the verb is correct, write *correct*.

1. Most Americans <u>drives</u> to work.   _____ drive _____

2. Many Americans <u>take</u> public transportation.   _____

3. Most American women <u>doesn't get</u> married before age 25.   _____

4. The average American <u>have</u> a computer.   _____

5. The average American <u>doesn't eat</u> a large breakfast.   _____

6. Most American families <u>has</u> one or two children.   _____

7. Americans <u>eats</u> their main meal in the evening.   _____

A **ACADEMIC** Take a class survey. Write the information about your class.

- One student is the leader and will read each question to the entire class.
- Students will raise their hands to show their answers to each question.
- Two students are the counters. They will count each answer, including their own.
- Write the answers in your book.

1. Number of students in our class: _____

2. Seat belts

    Who wears a seat belt? _____

    Who doesn't wear a seat belt? _____

3. Work

    Who works part time? _____

    Who works full time? _____

    Who doesn't work? _____

4. How many hours do you watch TV?

    Who doesn't watch TV? _____

    Who watches TV one hour a day? _____

    Who watches TV two hours a day? _____

    Who watches TV three hours a day? _____

    Who watches TV four or more hours a day? _____

5. What country are you from?

Country	Number of Students
_____	_____
_____	_____
_____	_____
_____	_____
_____	_____
_____	_____
_____	_____

B **ACADEMIC** In small groups, draw four charts to show the results of your class survey. Use the information from Exercise A.

WORKING AND SAVING

ACADEMIC Identify and retell key details; recall information

AT WORK Describe occupations; ask and answer questions about employment and the workplace

CIVICS Learn about and discuss how to pay for college; understand money-saving tips; write an email to customer service

These men compare sections of counterfeit, or fake, one-hundred dollar bills to a sample of a real bill.

A baker stands behind shelves of baked goods.

A **AT WORK** Complete the sentences about bakers using the present.

1. A baker (train) _____trains_____ in bakeries, grocery stores, and restaurants.

2. Some bakers (study) _____ for one to two years at culinary or technical schools.

3. Other bakers (learn / sometimes) _____ on the job.

4. Bakers in training (prepare) _____ breads, pies, cookies, and other baked goods.

5. A baker (use) _____ mixers to prepare dough.

6. A new baker (learn) _____ the basics and correct sanitation procedures.

7. Bakers (work) _____ part time or full time.

8. Many bakers (work / often) _____ weekends and holidays.

B Discuss these questions.

1. Do you know how to bake? If you do, what do you like to bake?

2. Do you have a favorite bakery? Where is it?

3. What kind of baked goods do you like to eat?

Do	I you we they	work learn have	full time? on the job? long hours?
Does	he she		
	it	taste	good?

Yes, I **do**.	No, I **don't**.
Yes, you **do**.	No, you **don't**.
Yes, we **do**.	No, we **don't**.
Yes, they **do**.	No, they **don't**.
Yes, he **does**.	No, he **doesn't**.
Yes, she **does**.	No, she **doesn't**.
Yes, it **does**.	No, it **doesn't**.

A Read the conversation. Then, practice it with a partner.

Jack: Do you like your job?

Andrea: Yes, I do. I'm a baker.

Jack: Really? Do you work full time or part time?

Andrea: I work part time right now.

Jack: Do you work on weekends?

Andrea: Yes, I do. Weekends are very busy at the bakery.

B **LET'S TALK.** Walk around the classroom and ask the following questions about jobs. If a student answers "Yes," write that student's name. If a student answers "No," ask another student the question.

Questions	Student's Name
1. Do you have a job?	_____
2. Do you work full time?	_____
3. Do you like your job?	_____
4. Do you work weekends?	_____
5. Do you have benefits?	_____
6. Do you like your coworkers?	_____
7. Do you feel tired at the end of the day?	_____
8. Do you have to sign in at work?	_____
9. Do you want to find a different job?	_____

C **AT WORK** Complete the questions about radiation therapists.

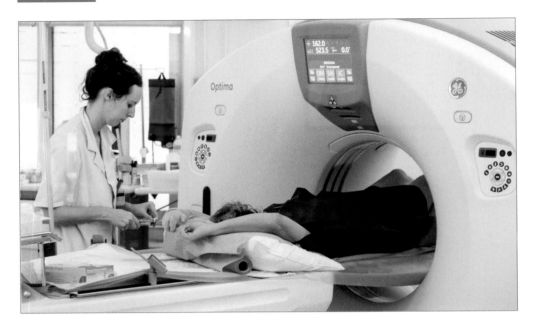

A **radiation therapist** uses radiation to treat patients with cancer and other diseases.

	Kendra	Mario and Lana
Education	has a bachelor's degree	have associate degrees
Place of work	works at a hospital	work at an outpatient center
Full time / Part time	works full time	work part time
Specialty	specializes in breast cancer	specialize in skin cancer
Salary	earns $102,500	earn $45,100 each
Savings	saves $1,000 a month	save $1,200 a month each

1. __Does__ Kendra __have__ a bachelor's degree? __Yes, she does.__

2. __Do__ Mario and Lana __have__ bachelor's degrees? __No, they don't.__

3. _____ Mario and Lana _____ associate degrees? _____

4. _____ Mario and Lana _____ at a hospital? _____

5. _____ Kendra _____ part time? _____

6. _____ Mario and Lana _____ part time? _____

7. _____ Mario and Lana _____ in skin cancer? _____

8. _____ Kendra _____ in skin cancer? _____

9. _____ Kendra _____ a good salary? _____

10. _____ Mario and Lana _____ a lot of money each month? _____

ACTIVE GRAMMAR | Present: *Wh-* Questions

What Where When Why How How often How much How many hours	**do**	I you we they	**work?** **study?** **save?**
	does	he she	
		it	**last?**

A bank teller.

A Match the questions and answers about Liza, a bank teller.

___i___ **1.** Where does a bank teller work?   **a.** At 6:30 a.m.

_____ **2.** What does a bank teller do?   **b.** Yes, she does.

_____ **3.** What time does Liza get up?   **c.** A dress or a suit.

_____ **4.** How does she get to work?   **d.** At 9:00 a.m.

_____ **5.** What does she wear to work?   **e.** She takes the bus.

_____ **6.** What time does the bank open?   **f.** She earns $31,000 a year.

_____ **7.** What benefits does she get?   **g.** A teller handles cash and helps customers.

_____ **8.** What time does the bank close?   **h.** Medical benefits.

_____ **9.** How much does she earn?   **i.** A bank teller works at a bank.

_____ **10.** Does she like her job?   **j.** At 4:00 p.m.

B Write questions about a bank security guard. Ask and answer the questions with a partner. Use your imagination to answer the questions.

1. Where _____?

2. How many hours _____?

3. What time _____?

4. How much _____?

5. What _____?

C **ACADEMIC** Listen and take notes about how Laura spends money each day. Laura works at a bakery and would like to save more of her paycheck. Add up the total. 🎧11

Expenses	Amount
Coffee and donut	$4.00
Total	

D Complete the questions about Laura's daily expenses.

1. What _____ does Laura buy at the coffee shop _____? A coffee and a donut

2. How far _____? About a mile

3. Why _____? Because she gets up late

4. How much _____? About $8.00

5. What _____? A soda

6. How much _____? $4.00 a day

7. What _____? A lottery ticket

8. _____? No, she doesn't have a budget.

E Read the conversation. Then, write a conversation about some of your daily or weekly expenses. Use some of the ideas in the word box. Present your conversation to the class.

A: Do you know how you spend your money?

B: Not really.

A: How do you get to work?

B: I drive. I spend about $20 a week on gas.

A: How much do you spend a day on lunch?

B: I usually spend six or seven dollars.

A: What else do you buy every day?

B: I always get a cup of coffee on my way to work.

bus / train
childcare
clothes
coffee
gas
lottery tickets
lunch

F **LET'S TALK.** Write questions about Marta and Ryan's activities and expenses. Then, work in a group and ask and answer your questions.

1. apartment
2. rent: $1,000 a month

3. three times a week
4. from 6:00 to 7:00

5. college / part time
6. Tuesday and Thursday

7. a salesman
8. gas: $3,000 a year

9. every Saturday night
10. Thai

11. savings: $100 a month

1. _Where do they live?_ _____

2. _How much do they pay for rent?_ _____

3. How often _____

4. How long _____

5. Does _____

6. When _____

7. What _____

8. How much _____

9. How often _____

10. What kind of food _____

11. How much _____

When *who* is the subject of a sentence, it is always singular.		When *who* is the object of a sentence, it can be singular or plural.	
Who works at City Bank?	**Liza** does.	**Who** does he drive to work?	He drives **his brother** to work.
Who saves money every month?	**Henry and Ivan** do.	**Who** do they send money to?	They send money **to their parents**.

A **LET'S TALK.** In a group, answer the questions. Then, make sentences about your group.

1. Who has young children?
2. Who lives in an apartment?
3. Who has a mortgage?
4. Who banks online?
5. Who buys lottery tickets?
6. Who downloads music?
7. Who works at night?

B Write questions with *Who* about each statement.

1. Molly drives her daughter to school.

   _____*Who does Molly drive to school*_____?

2. Nidia wants to be a nurse.

   _____*Who wants to be a nurse*_____?

3. Josh saves $100 a week.

   _____?

4. Carlos calls his girlfriend every night.

   _____?

5. Martin sends money to his brother every month.

   _____?

6. Sofia belongs to a health club.

   _____?

7. Wendy works the night shift.

   _____?

Yes / No Questions with *be*

Am	I	
Are	you we they	**tired**? **a student**? **at school**?
Is	he she	
	it	**cheap**?

Yes / No Questions with *do*

Do	I you we they	**work**	in a bank? at night?
Does	he she		
	it	**cost**	a lot?

When asking a *Yes / No* question, use *be* with adjectives and nouns. Use *do / does* with verbs other than *be*.

A Complete the questions with *Am*, *Are*, *Is*, *Do*, or *Does*.

1. _____Do_____ you have a credit card?

2. _____Does_____ he spend a lot of money?

3. _____Am_____ I careful with my money?

4. _____ she sometimes late with her bills?

5. _____ he work full time?

6. _____ gas expensive?

7. _____ you shop at the mall every weekend?

8. _____ they pay taxes?

9. _____ you good at saving money?

10. _____ your family compare prices?

B With a partner, ask and answer the questions.

Do you work in a bank?   No, I don't.

1. you / work in a bank?

2. you / get up early in the morning?

3. you / a serious student?

4. your teacher / from the United States?

5. this class / difficult?

6. you / talkative?

7. your teacher / give a lot of homework?

8. you / always do your homework?

A Discuss the meanings of these words with your class.

3D design	animation
character	design
internship	technology

> An **internship** is a program for beginners in an occupation at an organization. An internship may last a summer, a semester, or a year. **Interns** are often students or recent graduates.

B Listen to Mia's story. Then, complete the information about Mia's background and internship. 🎧12

1. Mia is a student at a university in _____ Pennsylvania _____.

2. She is studying design, _____, and _____.

3. She wants to design _____ for _____ games.

4. She has experience with computer _____ and 3D _____.

5. She has a paid _____ internship. She will work 40 hours a week.

6. Her pay is _____ a month.

7. Her _____ at the university is very expensive.

C **ACADEMIC** Write questions about Mia.

1. Why _____ *does Mia need to save money* _____?

She needs to save money because tuition is expensive.

2. How _____?

She feels excited.

3. Who _____?

She works with a team of people.

4. What _____ every morning?

She buys coffee and breakfast.

5. Where _____?

She stops at a coffee shop on the way to work.

6. What _____ at night?

She rents a movie or goes out with the other interns.

7. _____?

Yes, she does.

D Write three more questions about Mia. Ask a classmate your questions.

1. _____

2. _____

3. _____

E **LET'S TALK.** With a small group of students, list other ways that Mia can save money.

1. _____

2. _____

3. _____

4. _____

A Discuss these questions.

1. How much does college cost? Do all colleges cost the same?

2. How do students pay for college?

B **CIVICS** Read and discuss the information about paying for college.

Paying for College

College in the United States is very expensive. However, there are several ways to pay for tuition and fees. To access many of the financial aid opportunities available, students do not need to be US citizens: these opportunities are also open to permanent residents and refugees. High school students can speak with a counselor. People who have finished high school can contact the college that they want to attend. Here are a few options that help students pay for college:

Federal Grants

Many students are eligible for federal grants. Some grants are need-based and help low-income students. Other grants are merit-based and are for students with high grades. Students do not need to pay back grants. They must attend school at least part time. Students can apply for federal grants online.

Scholarships

A scholarship is money that a student receives based on need, high grades, athletic ability, or other criteria. Colleges, local organizations, and businesses give scholarships. Ask the financial aid office or go online to find a list of scholarships that are available.

Tuition Reimbursement

Many businesses help their workers pay for college. In most cases, an employee registers and takes a class at a college. When the employee passes the course, usually with a C grade or better, the employer pays back all or part of the tuition. Check your company's benefits and policies.

Federal Student Loans

The federal government offers student loans with low interest rates. Students do not need to pay back the loan until they finish college. They must pay back the money with interest whether they finish college or not. Students can apply for a federal loan online. 🎧13

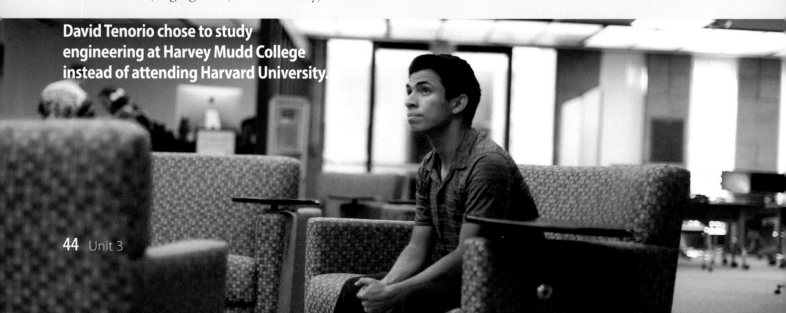

David Tenorio chose to study engineering at Harvey Mudd College instead of attending Harvard University.

C Check the information that applies for each type of financial assistance.

Type of Assistance	Students with Need	Students with Good Grades	Federal Program	Must Pay Back
Grants				
Scholarships				
Tuition Reimbursement				
Student Loans				

D Read and discuss the information about student loan repayment.

After students finish or stop attending college, they must start paying back their student loans plus interest. The standard repayment plan is for ten years, one payment a month, 120 payments in all.

Karla, Josh, and Deanna all borrowed money to attend college at a 4.45% interest rate.

Karla borrowed $6,000. She attended college for a year but stopped attending after that.

Josh borrowed $10,000 to attend a two-year college.

Derek borrowed $50,000 to attend a four-year college.

	Karla	Josh	Derek
Total amount borrowed	$6,000	$10,000	$50,000
Interest amount at end of loan	$1,462	$4,873	$12,183
Total amount to pay back	$7,462	$14,873	$62,183
Monthly payment for ten years	$62	$207	$518

E Answer the questions about the loan information in the chart above.

1. What is the interest rate on each loan? _____
2. Does Karla have to pay back her loan? _____
3. What is her monthly payment? _____
4. How much did Josh borrow? _____
5. How much is his monthly payment? _____
6. How much did Derek borrow? _____
7. What is the total amount he has to pay back? _____
8. How much is his monthly payment? _____

F **LET'S TALK.** In a group, agree or disagree with the following statements. Give your reasons.

1. If you don't have enough money, do not apply to college.
2. You should check how much money different careers pay.

A Discuss these questions. Have you ever sent an email to a business? Why did you send it?

B Read the following email to customer service.

To: customerservice@online*shop.com ◄── Put the recipient's email here. **Recipient** is another word for the person who receives the message.

Subject: Order #187653-445 ◄── If you have a complaint or a return, include the order number.

To Whom It May Concern: ◄── If you do not have a name, type *To Whom It May Concern*:

On January 5th, I ordered 12 rolls of paper towels for $28.97 and 2 boxes of 13-gallon kitchen trash bags for $23.30. The order total was $52.27 plus shipping and handling. The order arrived on January 8th, and I received only 6 rolls of paper towels and only 1 box of trash bags, but I was charged the full amount. Please credit my account, or send me the remaining part of my order. Please credit my credit card for any shipping and handling. Attached are the original order (#187653-445) and the packing slip that was in the box.

Thank you for your attention to this matter. If you need additional information, I can be reached at this email address or at (555) 555-1212.

Sincerely, ◄── End your email with *Sincerely*.

Charles Anton ◄── Include your full name.

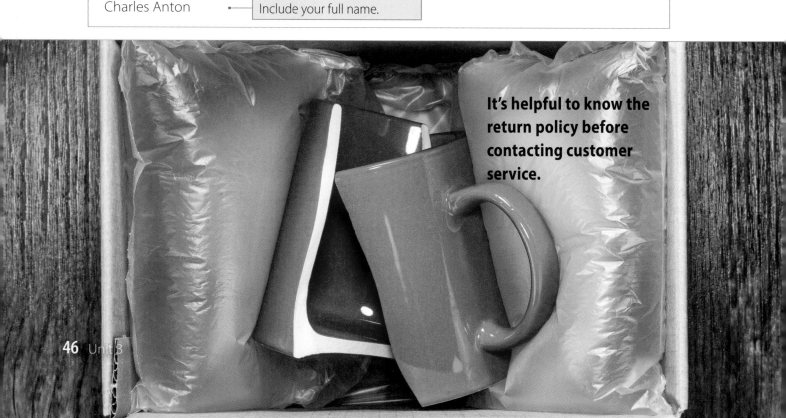

It's helpful to know the return policy before contacting customer service.

C Answer the questions.

1. Who wrote the email? _____ *Charles Anton* _____

2. When did he buy the products? _____

3. Did he buy the products from a store? _____

4. Why is he sending an email to the company? _____

_____

5. What does he want the company to do? _____

_____

6. Did he attach anything to the email? _____

_____

WRITING NOTE
Use capitals for:

the names of streets	the names of cities
the names of states	the first letter in every line of an address

D **CIVICS** Write an email to a company. Use one of the suggestions below or think of another reason.

1. You want to return a product.

2. Your credit card company made a mistake on your bill.

3. The cellphone company charged you for services you did not use.

4. You want to thank a business for excellent service.

5. You want to order a product or request information.

6. You purchased an object online, but it broke before you received it and you want a full refund.

WRITING NOTE
Emails to Customer Service
1. Use a clear subject.
2. Start your message with a greeting.
3. Make sure the email is brief and clear.
4. Use proper spelling, punctuation, and capitalization. Do not write the entire message using capital letters.
5. Mention any attachments that you send with the message.

A Read the article. Then, discuss the meanings of the words in bold with a partner.

In 1980, Omar got his first job. His monthly salary was $800. His parents told him, "Put 10 percent of your paycheck away for your future." Omar put $80 in the bank each month. Over the years, Omar's salary continued to rise, and he continued to save 10 percent of his salary. His next employer had a 401(k) plan. Omar continued to save 10 percent of his salary and his employer added 3 percent. When Omar retired last year, he had $475,000 in his 401(k) retirement plan!

How do people save money? Omar's **system** was simple—put 10 percent of every paycheck into a retirement plan. Here are some savings **tips** from money experts.

1. **Keep a budget.** This is the first step in any savings plan. How much money comes in every month? Where does it go? For a few months, keep a **record** of your expenses—car payments, gas, phone, rent, utility bills, food, and eating out. Don't forget about the large yearly **expenses** like car insurance.

2. **Make a plan.** Decide what you are saving for. A car? A house? Retirement? How much money do you need for each?

3. **Use your credit card wisely.** When you use credit cards, pay them off as soon as possible. If you pay $1,200 in credit card interest a year, that is $1,200 you could save.

4. **Buy used.** It is possible to buy lightly used items for half or less of the original price. Stop at garage sales and look for furniture and children's items. There are websites for used items in excellent condition. Car dealers offer late-model used cars with one-year warranties. These cars often have low mileage.

5. **Cut your spending.** Try to figure out how to **cut** your expenses. If you have a cellphone, can you drop your landline? Can you refinance your mortgage? Can you get a better price on car insurance? Do you need two cars?

Saving money is a family **effort**. Sit down with your partner and talk about money. As you start to save, you will feel more secure and satisfied as your dollars start to grow.

B **CIVICS** Search online for a basic budget worksheet. Use the keywords below. Print and bring several worksheets to class. Compare the worksheets and decide which is the most useful.

| free budget worksheet | basic budget planner | basic budget form |

A national park service worker at Mt. Rushmore, South Dakota.

ACADEMIC Read and understand maps; categorize nouns; find supporting details; write a report; prepare a presentation; make observations

AT WORK Listen to and give a presentation

CIVICS Identify land features in a map of the United States; learn about Montana, California, and the Death Valley National Park

canyon

waterfall

river

Palouse Falls State Park, Washington.

A Check the words you see in the photo. Look up the words you don't know.

B Give an example of each of these geographical features in the United States: a lake, a river, a mountain range, a seaport, an island, and a canyon.

C Circle *True* or *False* about your city.

1.	We can see mountains from our school.	True	False
2.	This city / town is on a river.	True	False
3.	If I drive for an hour, I can see the Atlantic or the Pacific Ocean.	True	False
4.	This city is the capital of the state.	True	False
5.	There is a desert near here.	True	False
6.	This city / town is near a lake.	True	False
7.	There is a large forest near here.	True	False
8.	This city / town is also a seaport.	True	False

ACTIVE GRAMMAR | Count Nouns: Singulars and Plurals

> **Count nouns** are people, places, or things that we can count individually (one by one).
> Count nouns can be singular or plural.
> Expressions with *one of the*, *every*, and *each* before the noun take a singular verb.
>   **Every** state **has** a capitol building.
> Expressions with *a few of the*, *some of the*, *many of the*, *all of the*, etc., take a plural verb.
>   **All of the** states **have** capitol buildings.

A Write *S* next to the nouns that take a singular verb, and *P* next to the nouns that take a plural verb.

1. _S_ a desert
2. _P_ mountains
3. _____ a forest
4. _____ rivers
5. _____ seaports

6. _____ one of the cities
7. _____ a mountain range
8. _____ a few of the parks
9. _____ every national park
10. _____ many of the people

11. _____ each of the farms
12. _____ all of the states
13. _____ millions of tourists
14. _____ every state
15. _____ several of the islands

B Circle the correct forms of the verbs.

1. A plain **is** / **are** a large area of flat land.
2. A range **is** / **are** a group of mountains.
3. Canyons **is** / **are** long, deep cracks in the earth's surface.
4. Glaciers **is** / **are** large rivers of slow-moving ice.
5. Every major city **has** / **have** a lot of traffic.
6. Many rivers **begins** / **begin** in the mountains.
7. Millions of tourists **visits** / **visit** national parks every summer.
8. Every dairy farm **produces** / **produce** milk.
9. Every state **has** / **have** interesting places to visit.
10. All the states **has** / **have** interesting places to visit.
11. Each farm **grows** / **grow** many kinds of vegetables.
12. All road maps **shows** / **show** cities and highways.
13. Most cities **has** / **have** skyscrapers.

One World Trade Center is a skyscraper in New York City.

C **Pronunciation: Syllables and stress** Listen and repeat. 🎧14

1. the At·lán·tic Ó·cean
2. the Ap·pa·lá·chian Móun·tains
3. the Mis·sis·síp·pi Rí·ver

D Listen and mark the stress. 🎧15

1. Ca·na·da
2. Mex·i·co
3. the U·ni·ted States
4. the Rock·y Moun·tains
5. the Grand Can·yon
6. A·las·ka
7. Ha·wai·i
8. the Pa·ci·fic O·cean
9. Death Val·ley

E Listen and point to each location on the map of the United States. 🎧16

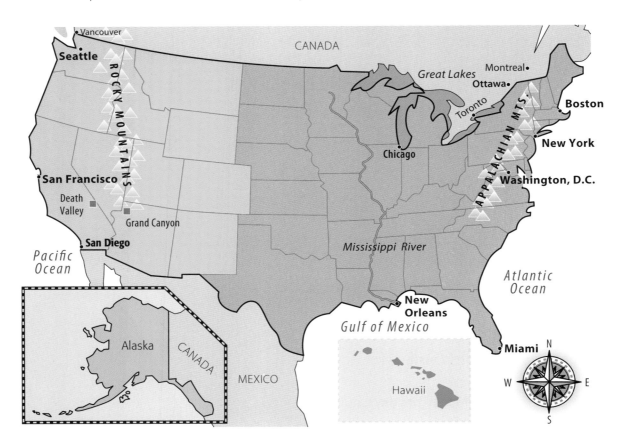

ACTIVE GRAMMAR | Quantifiers with Count Nouns

There	is isn't	**a**	seaport desert	on the coast.
	are	**a few** **several** **many** **a lot of**	seaports mountains rivers forests	in the North. in the South. in the East. in the West. in the central part of the country.
	aren't	**any**	farms	

A **CIVICS** Make sentences about the map on the previous page.

> There are many seaports on the coast.

> There is a high mountain range in the West.

1. countries
2. major cities
3. seaports
4. mountain ranges
5. large lakes
6. farms
7. major river
8. deserts
9. national parks

B **LET'S TALK.** With a partner, plan the perfect island. On the blank map, draw the features you would like, such as mountains, a river, a lake, and farms. Then, describe your island to another group.

> There is a small seaport town in the east. To the north of the seaport is a plain; there are a few farms there.

ACTIVE GRAMMAR | Count and Noncount Nouns

> **Count nouns** are items that we can count individually (one by one): lake—lakes. They can be singular or plural.
>
> **Noncount nouns** cannot be counted. They are always singular.
>
> **1.** Liquids or gases: water, oil, oxygen, rain
> **2.** Items that are too small or too numerous to count: sand, corn, rice
> **3.** General categories: traffic, scenery, music, tourism
> **4.** Ideas: information, beauty, work
>
> **Note:** Some words can be both count and noncount: crime—crimes, industry—industries.

A **ACADEMIC** Write the words under the correct column in the chart.

country	mountain	ranch	tourism
crime	museum	river	tourist
factory	noise	seaport	traffic
farm	pollution	skyscraper	unemployment
industry	rain	snow	university

Count Nouns	Noncount Nouns
industry	industry
mountain	pollution
tourist	unemployment

WORD PARTNERSHIPS	
air	
water	pollution
noise	

There	is	**no** **a little** **a lot of**	traffic pollution rain	in this city. in my country. in the United States.
	isn't	**any** **much**	crime industry	

A Complete the sentences. Use *there is*, *there isn't*, *there are*, or *there aren't*.

1. _____There are_____ a lot of factories in the city, so _____there is_____ a lot of pollution.

2. _____ a lot of traffic in the city, so _____ a lot of noise.

3. _____ a lot of large companies in the city, so _____ much unemployment.

4. _____ a large seaport near the city, so _____ a lot of traffic in the bay.

5. _____ many museums, restaurants, and shows, so _____ a lot of tourism.

6. _____ many police officers, so _____ much crime.

B Talk about the city or town that your school is in.

> There are a few colleges and universities near here.

> There is a lot of tourism in this city.

1. colleges and universities
2. tourism
3. factories
4. crime
5. museums
6. ethnic restaurants

7. traffic
8. nightclubs
9. unemployment
10. fast-food restaurants
11. noise
12. hospitals

ACTIVE GRAMMAR | *How many / How much*

How many	museums parks	are	there	in your city? in your country?
How much	snow traffic	is		

A **LET'S TALK.** Complete the questions. Use *How much* or *How many*. Then, in small groups, talk about the countries you come from. If possible, each student should be from a different country.

1. What country are you from?

2. ____How many____ skyscrapers are there in your country?

3. _____ tourism is there in your country?

4. _____ traffic is there in your country?

5. _____ immigrants are there in your country?

6. _____ farms are there in your country?

7. _____ snow is there in your country?

8. _____ mountain ranges are there in your country?

9. _____ crime is there in your country?

10. _____ universities are there in your country?

> I'm from Japan. There are many skyscrapers in my country.

B **STUDENT TO STUDENT.** Ask and answer questions about Canada and Mexico. Use *How much* and *How many*.

Student 1: Turn to Appendix C. Ask your partner about Canada. Complete the chart.

Student 2: Ask your partner about Mexico. Complete the chart below.

	Mexico	Canada
Tourism		a lot
Desert regions		one
Mountains		many
National parks		47
Snow		a lot
Ski resorts		many
Official languages		two

> How much tourism is there in Mexico?

> There is a lot of tourism in Mexico.

There	is	**too much** **not enough**	rain. industry.
	are	**too many** **not enough**	fast-food restaurants. parks.

We often use *not enough* and *too many / too much* to talk about problems or to complain.

not enough = less than you want or need

There are**n't enough** farms in that country. There is**n't enough** food.

too many, too much = more than you want or need

There are **too many** cars on the road. There is **too much** traffic.

A Listen to the complaints about world problems. Complete the sentences. Use the words in the box. 🎧 17

aren't enough	are too many	isn't enough	is too much

1. There ___isn't enough___ rain.

2. There _____ jobs.

3. There _____ homeless people.

4. There _____ food for everyone.

5. There _____ snow.

6. There _____ traffic.

7. There _____ public transportation.

8. There _____ plastic bottles.

B **ACADEMIC** **LET'S TALK.** In a group, make a list of five things you like and five things you don't like about the area where you live.

> There are a lot of good restaurants.

> There is too much crime.

Things we like	Things we don't like
1.	1.
2.	2.
3.	3.
4.	4.
5.	5.

A **CIVICS** Discuss the map of Montana.

1. What are Montana's borders?

2. What is the capital?

3. What geographical features do you see on this map?

B **ACADEMIC** Look at the map and listen. As you listen, point to each location on the map. Then, make statements. Use the words in the box. 🎧 **18**

GENERAL AND SPECIFIC STATEMENTS

General statements:
   There is a large national park in Montana.
Specific statements:
   Glacier National Park is in Montana.
Do not say: There is Glacier National Park in Montana.

Canada	Helena	national park	rain	the Missouri River
Fort Peck Lake	horse ranches	Native American reservations	rivers	the Rocky Mountains
Glacier National Park	lakes	Native Americans	snow	tourism

C Circle the letter of the correct answer.

1. What is to the north of Montana?
   a. Wyoming   **b.** Canada   **c.** Glacier National Park

2. What is the weather like in the western part of Montana?
   a. It's cold and wet.   **b.** It's cold and dry.   **c.** It's hot and wet.

3. What is the weather like in the eastern part of Montana?
   a. It's cold and wet.   **b.** It's cold and dry.   **c.** It's hot and dry.

4. Why is the eastern part of Montana dry?
   a. Because it is so far north.   **b.** Because the mountains stop the clouds.

5. Where are there many horse ranches?
   a. in the eastern part of the state   **b.** in the western part of the state

6. What is one of Montana's major industries?
   a. fishing   **b.** manufacturing   **c.** tourism

D Complete the sentences. Use the correct form of the verb.

1. The Missouri River (begin) _____begins_____ in Montana.

2. The western part of Montana (receive) _____ a lot of snow.

3. Montana (have) _____ very cold winters.

4. Thousands of tourists (visit) _____ Montana each year.

5. The Rocky Mountains (stop) _____ the rain clouds.

6. Many Native Americans (live) _____ on reservations.

7. Snow (cover) _____ the mountains.

E Listen and write the questions you hear. Then, ask and answer the questions with a partner. 🎧 19

1. How many _____

2. How many _____

3. _____

4. _____

5. _____

6. _____

DEATH VALLEY

Death Valley National Park is the largest national park in the continental United States. This 3.4-million-acre park in southern California is the lowest, hottest, and driest place in North America. The lowest point is 282 feet (86 meters) below **sea level**. In the summer, the average temperature is often higher than 120° (49° Celsius), and the highest temperature ever recorded there was 134° (56.6° Celsius). There are some summers when Death Valley receives no rain, and the average yearly **precipitation** is less than two inches.

A What do you know about deserts? Circle *True* or *False*.

1. A desert receives very little rain.	True	False
2. The only plants in the desert are different kinds of cactuses.	True	False
3. Animals cannot live in the desert.	True	False
4. Summer is the best time to visit the desert.	True	False

B ▶ **WATCH** Watch the video. Check your answers in Exercise A.

C Match.

___f___ **1.** sea level

_____ **2.** precipitation

_____ **3.** varieties

_____ **4.** roots

_____ **5.** adapt

_____ **6.** avoid

_____ **7.** exhibit

a. a show or display of art, plants, or animals

b. to change or adjust to new conditions

c. rain or snow

d. the parts of the plant that grow into the earth and brings in water

e. to stay away from

f. at the same height as the sea or ocean

g. kinds or types

READING NOTE

Supporting Details

When an article makes a statement, it usually gives specific information to support the statement.

The Timbisha Shoshone Tribe of Native Americans has lived in this desert area for hundreds of years.

In 1849, people heard about the discovery of gold in California. Thousands of people began the long trip to the West. This large desert area was so difficult to cross that some travelers looking for gold gave it the name Death Valley.

Today, tourists from all over the United States travel to Death Valley to enjoy its natural beauty. There are over one thousand **varieties** of plants in this desert, including many kinds of cactuses and flowers. Cactuses, with their interesting and unusual shapes, need very little rain. Their **roots** are close to the surface of the ground so they can quickly collect any rainfall. A few days after the first rain in the spring, thousands of wildflowers cover the desert.

There are also many animals that have learned to **adapt** to this hot climate. Most are active at night, sleeping during the day to **avoid** the hot desert sun. Some animals live their entire lives without drinking any water, getting water from the food they eat.

If you are planning a trip to Death Valley, winter is the best time to visit. The main visitor area has nature **exhibits**, a museum, and a bookstore. Be sure to watch the informative videos on desert life. After that, you can explore the desert by car, by bike, or on foot. Park rangers offer programs on desert life, the history of Death Valley, and the desert sky at night. If you are planning a trip to Death Valley, don't forget these four essentials: a sun hat, sun block, a lot of water, and a camera. 🎧 **20**

D **ACADEMIC** Write a detail from the reading to support each fact.

Statement	Supporting Detail
1. Death Valley is the largest park in the continental United States.	**1.** It is a 3.4-million-acre park.
2. It is the lowest place in North America.	**2.**
3. It is the hottest place in North America.	**3.**
4. It is the driest place in North America.	**4.**

E Match the two parts of each sentence.

_c_ **1.** Visitors need to bring sun block

_____ **2.** Summer is not the best time to visit Death Valley

_____ **3.** Desert animals are active at night

_____ **4.** Cactus roots are near the surface

_____ **5.** This area was named Death Valley

_____ **6.** After the first spring rain,

a. because it is cooler at this time.

b. because it was very difficult to cross.

c. to protect their skin from the sun.

d. millions of wildflowers cover the desert.

e. because it is very hot.

f. to quickly collect rainwater.

A **CIVICS** Read the student report about California.

A beach in La Jolla, California.

California is on the west coast of the United States and it's the third-largest state. It has borders with Oregon to the north, Nevada and Arizona to the east, Mexico to the south, and the Pacific Ocean to the west. Sacramento is its capital. The population is about forty million.

California is a beautiful state. Its coast has hundreds of miles of beautiful beaches. There are two mountain ranges in California, the Sierra Nevada in the east and the Coast Ranges along the Pacific. There are several deserts in the southeast.

Two of the major cities are San Francisco and Los Angeles. San Francisco is on the hills over San Francisco Bay. Tourists visit Chinatown and ride up and down the hills on the cable cars. Los Angeles is in southern California. It is the home of Hollywood and the movie industry.

For most of the year, the weather along the coast is sunny and mild. In the winter, there is snow in the mountains. In the south, the weather is hot and dry.

Agriculture and tourism are two of the major industries. California grows more than half of the nation's fruits and vegetables. Also, many Californians work in the tourist industry in the cities, parks, and resorts.

B **ACADEMIC** Write a report.

1. Choose a state in the United States. Each student should choose a different state.
2. Draw a map of the state. Show the borders, the capital, and major geographical features.
3. Complete the chart below. Look up information online.
4. Write a short report. You will use this information later for a class presentation.

State	
Location	
Borders	
Capital	
Population	
Geography	
Two major cities	
Weather	
Industries	

WRITING NOTE

Capital Letters
Use capital letters for the names of specific locations and geographical features:

Country names: the **U**nited **S**tates, **M**exico

State names: **A**laska, **N**ew **Y**ork

City names: **C**hicago, **S**an **D**iego

Bodies of water: the **P**acific **O**cean

Mountain ranges: the **R**ocky **M**ountains

Parks: **G**rand **C**anyon **N**ational **P**ark

Tourist attractions: the **S**tatue of **L**iberty

C Edit the paragraph.

　　Florida is the most popular tourist destination in the <u>U</u>nited states. During the winter, visitors enjoy a break from the cold and snow. Florida offers hundreds of miles of beaches along the atlantic ocean and the gulf of mexico. Families enjoy tourist attractions, such as disney world, universal studios, and sea world. Cities in Florida, such as miami, tampa, and fort lauderdale, offer great restaurants and exciting night life. Florida's most popular park is everglades national park, where visitors can birdwatch, fish or take boat tours, and see alligators and crocodiles.

ENGLISH IN ACTION / Giving a Class Presentation

A **ACADEMIC** Read the steps for giving a successful class presentation about the state you researched.

1. Prepare your materials: large map, notes, two or three photos from the internet.
2. Practice your presentation.
3. Stand in front of the class and look at your classmates.
4. Use your notes, but do not read directly from them.
5. Speak loudly, clearly, and slowly.
6. Show the map to the class. Tell your classmates the name of the state and explain the location.
7. Point to the capital. Spell the capital. Tell the class the population of the state.
8. Point to two places of interest on the map. Tell the class one or two things that people can enjoy at each location as you show the class your photos.

B Listen to one student's report. Discuss the questions. 🎧 21

1. How did this student prepare?
2. How large was the map? Could the students see the words on the map?
3. How many times did the student repeat the population?
4. What two places of interest did the student talk about?
5. How long was the presentation?
6. How do you feel when you stand in front of a group?
7. How can you best prepare to talk in front of the class?

C **AT WORK** Give a classroom presentation about the state you researched. As you listen to your classmates' presentations, take notes about each state.

State: _____

Capital: _____

Population: _____

An interesting fact: _____

> I researched Ohio. Ohio has a population of…

> Here's the capital of…

UNIT 5 TECHNOLOGY

A photographer uses a camera with flash bulbs to take a photo in the 1930s.

ACADEMIC Give and follow directions; identify the topic of a paragraph; identify key details in a text

AT WORK Understand the impact of technology on a business

CIVICS Discuss how technology has changed everyday life; read and understand signs

A Label the electronic equipment.

| fitness tracker | laptop | tablet |
| game console | smartphone | virtual reality headset |

1. _____

2. _____

3. _____

4. _____

5. _____

6. _____

B Complete the sentences. Then, discuss your answers.

1. I **have / don't have** a laptop.

2. I **have / don't have** internet access at home.

3. The school **has / doesn't have** a computer lab for students.

4. I spend about _____ hours a day on social media.

5. I have the following electronic device(s): _____

   _____

6. I'd like to buy the following electronic device(s): _____

7. I can use the following software: _____

8. My favorite social media site is _____

9. My favorite app is _____

I	**am**		send**ing** an email.
You	**are**		order**ing** a pizza.
He She	**is**	(not)	mak**ing** reservations.
It	**is**		work**ing**.
We They	**are**		play**ing** a video game.

1. The present continuous talks about an action that is happening now.
   He **is using** his computer.
2. The present continuous talks about an action that is temporary.
   He **is living** with his brother. (He expects to move soon.)

A Complete the sentences. Use the present continuous form of the verb.

1. Li-Ping (write) _____is writing_____ to her brother. She (email / not) _____ him. She (text) _____ him.

2. Raul (take) _____ a virtual tour of an art museum. He (look) _____ at paintings by Picasso and Dalí.

3. Mr. and Mrs. Chan (visit) _____ their friends in the city. They (stay / not) _____ in a hotel. They (stay) _____ with their friends.

4. Lauren (learn) _____ a new software program. She (take / not) _____ the course at her company. She (attend) _____ a local college.

B **CIVICS** Read each sign. Imagine that a person is breaking the rules. What is he or she doing?

1.
2.
3.
4.

5.
6.
7.
8.

That man isn't paying attention to the sign. He is taking a photo.

Am	I	tak**ing** a photo?
Are	you	send**ing** an email?
Is	he	read**ing** a book?
Is	she	listen**ing** to music?
Is	it	work**ing**?
Are	we	study**ing**?
Are	they	mak**ing** reservations?

Yes, you **are**.	No, you **aren't**.	No, you're not.
Yes, I **am**.	No, I'm **not**.	
Yes, he **is**.	No, he **isn't**.	No he's not.
Yes, she **is**.	No, she **isn't**.	No, she's not.
Yes, it **is**.	No, it **isn't**.	No, it's not.
Yes, we **are**.	No, we **aren't**.	No, we're not.
Yes, they **are**.	No, they **aren't**.	No, they're not.

A Ask and answer the questions with a partner.

> Are we sitting in the classroom?

> Yes, we are.

1. we / sit in the classroom?
2. you / speak your native language?
3. we / speak English?
4. teacher / take a break?
5. you / look out the window?

6. it / rain?
7. students / take a test?
8. we / look at our books?
9. we / sit in the back of the classroom?
10. you / drink water?

B Listen to each speaker. Ask questions and guess what he or she is doing. Then, listen again and compare your questions with a partner's. 🎧 **22**

1. Is he taking a photo? _____

2. _____

3. _____

4. _____

5. _____

6. _____

7. _____

ACTIVE GRAMMAR / Present Continuous: *Wh-* Questions

What	**am**	I	do**ing**?
Which movie	**are**	you	order**ing**?
How	**is**	it	work**ing**?
Where	**are**	they	go**ing**?

You're check**ing** prices.
I'm order**ing** *Space Age*.
It's work**ing** well.
They are go**ing** to the lab.

The present continuous can be used to talk about specific future plans.
I'**m leaving** at 2:00.

A Complete the questions.

Conversation 1

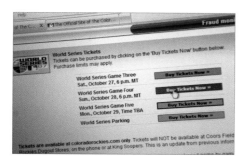

A: What website ___is___ he ___looking at___ ?
     ──1──   ─────2─────

B: He's looking at a sports ticket website.

A: What _____ he _____?
          ─3─   ────4────

B: He's buying a ticket to the World Series.

A: When _____ he _____?
          ─5─   ────6────

B: He's going on October 28th.

Conversation 2

A: What _____ ?
              ──1──

B: She's shopping for shoes.

A: What site _____?
                  ──2──

B: She's using Online Shop.

A: What kind of shoes _____?
                          ──3──

B: She's looking for shoes for work.

A: How many pairs _____?
                      ──4──

B: She's buying two pairs of shoes.

B Listen to the conversation. Then, practice it with a partner. 🎧 **23**

A: What are you doing?

B: I'm writing a report.

A: What software are you using?

B: I'm using Write Now.

A: How's it coming?

B: Very slowly. And it's due tomorrow.

C Pronunciation: *Wh-* questions Listen and repeat. 🎧24

1. Where is he going?
2. Who are you texting?
3. What is she studying?
4. Who is she calling?

5. What are you listening to?
6. Which game is she playing?
7. What are you ordering?
8. Which site are you using?

Wh- questions have a rising / falling intonation.

D LET'S TALK. In your notebook, write ten questions about the people in the picture. Then, in a group, ask and answer the questions.

What is Ahmed printing?

ACTIVE GRAMMAR | Present Continuous: *Who* Questions

When *Who* is the subject of a sentence, it is always singular.
Who is buying a computer?   Laura **is**.
Who is fixing the computer?   Henry and Ivan **are**.
When *Who* is the object of a sentence, it can be singular or plural.
Who is Max calling?   He **is** calling his sister.
Who are Ali and Kim talking to?   They **are** talking to their friends.

A Answer the questions. Use your imagination.

1. Who is taking a photo? _____ Mark is. _____
2. Who is he taking a photo of? _____ His daughter _____

3. Who is writing an email? _____
4. Who is she writing to? _____

5. Who is driving? _____
6. Who is taking a trip? _____

B **LET'S TALK.** Two or three students will act out each situation for the class. Ask two *Who* questions about each situation.

1. Student 1 is giving a book to Student 2.
2. Student 1 is taking a photo of two students.
3. Student 1 is helping Student 2 with homework.
4. Student 1 is inviting Student 2 to a party.
5. Student 1 is texting Student 2.
6. Three students are talking to the teacher.

Who is Lynn giving a book to?

Who is giving a book to Martha?

Some verbs in English do not usually take the present continuous. They are called **nonaction verbs**. These verbs often refer to the senses, to feelings, or to beliefs, or they show possession.

agree	hate	love	seem
believe	have	need	smell
belong	hear	own	sound
cost	know	prefer	taste
feel	like	remember	think
forget	look	see	understand

Some verbs can show both action and nonaction.

I have a computer.
I think he's a good teacher.

I'm having a good time.
She's having a party.
I'm thinking about my boyfriend.

More information in Appendix A.

A Complete the sentences. Use the present or the present continuous form of the verb in parentheses.

1. Which weather app (prefer) _____*do*_____ you _____*prefer*_____?

2. I (remember / not) _____ my password for this site.

3. I (try) _____ to find a good recipe for banana bread. This one (sound) _____ good.

4. They (save) _____ money to buy a computer. Their children (need) _____ one for school.

5. Hannah (sit) _____ at her computer. She (look) _____ confused. She (know / not) _____ how to use this software.

6. My sister (belong) _____ to her high school basketball team.

7. We (think / not) _____ that our car gets good gas mileage. We (look / not) _____ at SUVs or vans. We (think) _____ about buying a hybrid.

8. Our neighbor (have) _____ a party next week. (you / have) _____ an invitation?

9. I (listen / not) _____ to music. I (listen) _____ to a podcast.

10. That tablet (cost) _____ too much!

ACTIVE GRAMMAR | Simple Present and Present Continuous

Time Expressions with Present Continuous	Time Expressions with Simple Present	Adverbs of Frequency
now today at this moment at this time	once a day every day every morning all the time	always usually sometimes never

A Circle the correct time expression.

1. Linda is checking her email **now** / **in the morning**.

2. She receives about twenty emails **right now / every day**.

3. Shanta is listening to a podcast **now / every day**. She listens to the podcast **now / every morning**.

4. The students are putting their cellphones in their backpacks **right now / all the time**.

5. Sarah just finished her report for science. She is using spell check **right now / in the evening**.

6. Stanley is taking a break **at this moment / twice a day**. He's playing a card game.

7. My wi-fi isn't working very well **every day / right now**.

B **LET'S TALK.** In a group, write three sentences about what you are doing in class now. Then, write three sentences on a separate sheet of paper about what you do in class every day.

C Ask and answer the questions with a partner.

1. Do you have a computer?
2. Are you using a computer now?
3. Do you have a phone with you?
4. Are you talking on your phone?
5. Are you carrying a wallet?

6. Do you have a credit card?
7. Are you working with a partner?
8. Do you often work with a partner?
9. Are you writing now?
10. Are you talking with the teacher?

| Yes, I am.
No, I'm not. | Yes, I do.
No, I don't. |

A Technology is changing the way that people live and do business. Look at each photo. How do you think that the internet is changing each industry?

B **AT WORK** Listen to the ways that technology is changing businesses. 🎧 25

C Circle *True* or *False*.

1.	Technology is hurting some businesses.	True	False
2.	Most people make their airline reservations with a travel agent.	True	False
3.	There aren't many video rental stores.	True	False
4.	Many people watch movies at home.	True	False
5.	People are using apps to request rides.	True	False
6.	Taxi companies are hiring many new drivers.	True	False
7.	Online shopping is becoming more popular.	True	False
8.	It is difficult to compare prices online.	True	False

D CIVICS Explain how technology has changed the way people live.

1. People called a travel agent to make airline reservations.
   People are making airline reservations online.

2. People rented videos at a video store.
   _____

3. People called taxis for a ride.
   _____

4. People bought books in bookstores.
   _____

5. People looked at maps for directions.
   _____

6. People read print newspapers.
   _____

E Complete the questions in the present continuous.

1. What _____ *are you looking for* _____?
   I'm looking for a new vacuum cleaner.

2. Which site _____?
   I'm using a home improvement website.

3. Which movie _____?
   He's ordering the new superhero movie.

4. Who _____?
   A taxi is picking me up.

5. How _____ to the airport?
   She's getting to the airport by taxi.

6. Why _____?
   The store is closing because too many people are shopping online.

F LET'S TALK. In small groups, talk about the apps you use.

1. How do you listen to music?
2. What are your favorite shopping sites?
3. When you need transportation, which app do you use?
4. Which app do you use to communicate with your friends?
5. Where do you watch movies online?
6. Which travel apps do you use?
7. What is your favorite app? Tell your group how it works.

Technology Addiction

"Larry used to be an excellent student. Now, he's falling asleep in class. He's not completing his class work… He's always on the computer playing video games. Even at one and two o'clock in the morning, I can hear him playing video games in his room."   —A mother's report

1. An addiction is an activity or a habit that people cannot control and that is harmful to them. Psychologists are talking about a new kind of addiction—technology addiction. People with a technology addiction can't stop using their electronic devices—checking email and social media, playing video games, chatting, browsing the internet.

2. Do you know any technology addicts? Hours, or even days, pass, and they are still sitting at the computer or looking at their devices. They get upset when someone interrupts them. They feel nervous or depressed when they aren't on the computer, playing a video game, or using the internet. When they finally use their electronic devices again, they feel relieved. They neglect their family and friends.

3. If you think you are becoming addicted to technology, there are steps that you can take to limit your time using electronic devices.

- Set an alarm for one or two hours. When the alarm goes off, do an offline activity, like reading a book or exercising.

- Choose a time to disconnect from your electronic devices at night. For example, turn off your computer at 11:00 every night.

- Do other activities that you enjoy. Go out to lunch with friends, take a class, or exercise.

- If these ideas don't help, you might need professional help. 🎧 26

Technology is now always at our fingertips.

A Discuss these questions.

    1. How many hours a day do you spend on the computer?

    2. What are some examples of addictions?

B Circle the letter of each correct answer.

    1. Eating too much _____ is **harmful** to your health.

        a. fruit   **b.** junk food

    2. You **interrupt** someone who is reading when you _____.

        a. walk by quietly   **b.** start to talk to him or her

    3. You feel **relieved** when your teacher tells you that _____.

        a. you passed the test   **b.** you failed the test

    4. If you **neglect** your health, you _____.

        a. will get sick   **b.** will feel better

    5. If you **limit** the time you watch TV, you watch _____.

        a. more TV   **b.** less TV

C `ACADEMIC` Write the number of the correct paragraph next to the topic of the paragraph.

    ___2___ The signs of technology addiction

    _____ Ways to control technology addiction

    _____ The definition of technology addiction

> **READING NOTE**
>
> **Identifying the topic of a paragraph**
>
> The topic of a paragraph tells what the paragraph is about.

D `ACADEMIC` Answer the questions.

    1. Define technology addiction.

    _____

    _____

    2. What is one sign of technology addiction?

    _____

    _____

    3. What is one way to help a person limit the use of their devices?

    _____

    _____

WRITING OUR STORIES / An email

A Read the email message.

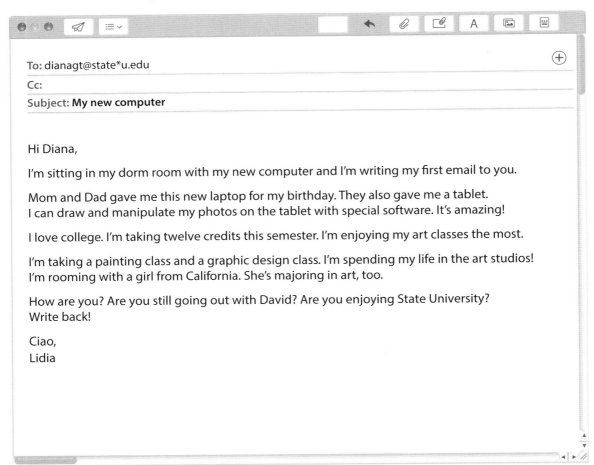

To: dianagt@state*u.edu

Cc:

Subject: **My new computer**

Hi Diana,

I'm sitting in my dorm room with my new computer and I'm writing my first email to you.

Mom and Dad gave me this new laptop for my birthday. They also gave me a tablet.
I can draw and manipulate my photos on the tablet with special software. It's amazing!

I love college. I'm taking twelve credits this semester. I'm enjoying my art classes the most.

I'm taking a painting class and a graphic design class. I'm spending my life in the art studios!
I'm rooming with a girl from California. She's majoring in art, too.

How are you? Are you still going out with David? Are you enjoying State University?
Write back!

Ciao,
Lidia

B **ACADEMIC** Answer the questions.

1. Who wrote this email?

_____

2. Who did she send the email to?

_____

3. What is the recipient's email address?

_____

4. What does *.edu* mean?

_____

5. What is Lidia majoring in?

_____

C Find and correct the mistakes with the simple present or present continuous.

1. She is ~~send~~ *sending* an email message.
2. She learning how to use new software.
3. The school have a computer lab.
4. She sits in the computer lab now.
5. You writing an email to your friend?
6. How everything with you?
7. What classes she is taking?
8. I'm preferring to use my tablet to a laptop.
9. She meet a lot of people.
10. You still going out with David?

WRITING NOTE

Check for spelling errors
After you write, use your computer's spell check to find any spelling errors.

D Write an email message to a friend or a classmate.

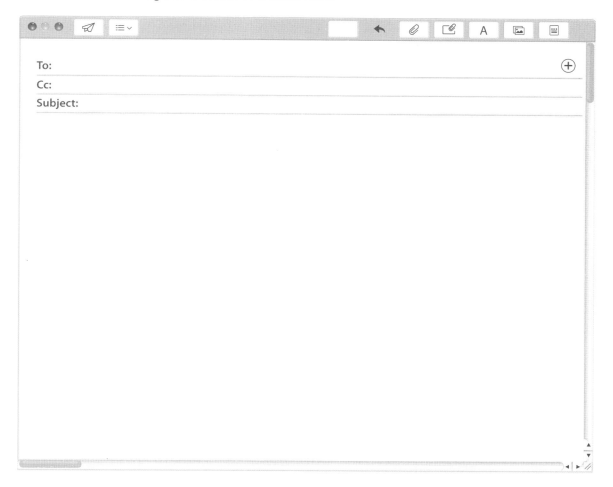

A Read the directions for setting an alarm on a cellphone. How are these directions the same or different for your phone?

> **To set an alarm:**
> 1. Tap the **clock** on the home screen.
> 2. Press the icon for **alarm**.
> 3. Touch **the plus sign**.
> 4. Enter the time you want the alarm to ring.
> 5. Select **a.m.** or **p.m.**
> 6. Press **Save** or **OK**.

B **ACADEMIC** Choose one of the features below or a favorite feature on your phone. In your notebook, give step-by-step directions on how to use the feature. Use words from the box to help you.

choose	enter	press	select	tap	touch

a. how to take a photo and email it to a friend

b. how to write a text message and send it

c. how to enter a new contact into your phone

d. how to enter a new event on your calendar

e. how to record a voice memo

f. how to use a map app to get directions

g. how to listen to music or watch a video

C **LET'S TALK.** Give your phone to a classmate. Carefully explain your directions. Can your partner follow your directions?

D Complete the information about your cellphone. Then, talk about the features you use most often.

1. I have a _____ phone.

2. I talk on my phone about _____ minutes a day.

3. My reception is **great / good / fair**.

4. My cellphone plan has these features. Check all that apply:

   ☐ It offers a family plan.   ☐ It has unlimited data.

   ☐ It has unlimited talk.   ☐ I can lease a phone.

   ☐ It has unlimited texting.   ☐ There is no fee for early termination.

E **LET'S TALK.** In a group of three, make a chart to compare your cellphone plans. Include the company name, number of phones, data limits, signal quality, and cost.

A HEALTHY LIFESTYLE

ACADEMIC Make inferences; make predictions; take a survey; organize ideas

AT WORK Describe tasks associated with healthcare professionals

CIVICS Understand what to do during a 911 call

Swimming is a fun way to stay active.

A AT WORK Discuss the pictures. Where is each person? What is happening? What else happens during a physical examination at the doctor's office?

check his blood pressure	fill a cavity	give a vaccine	read an eye chart
check his cholesterol	floss her teeth	have a physical	take an X-ray
examine	get a vaccine	order a test	write a prescription

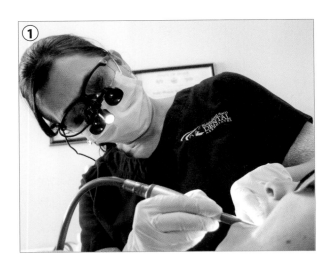

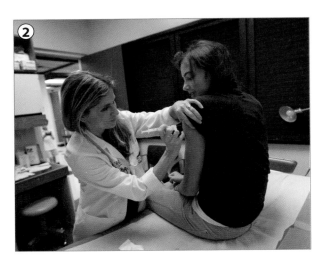

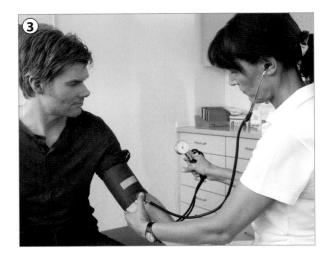

ACTIVE GRAMMAR | Future with *Be going to:* Statements

I	am			exercise.
You	are			**make** an appointment.
He She	is	(not)	going to	**call** the doctor.
We They	are			**take** medication.
It	is			**heal**.

A Read about Gloria. Underline each use of *be going to* plus verb.

Gloria is at the dentist. This is her first visit in two years. Gloria has four cavities. The doctor is filling two cavities today. He <u>is going to fill</u> two more cavities next week. Gloria is going to take better care of her teeth. She isn't going to drink soda with every meal. She isn't going to eat chocolate every day. She is going to floss her teeth every evening.

B Complete the sentences with the correct form of *be going to*.

1. I (go) _____ *am going to go* _____ to the dentist next week.

2. Many people (get) _____ flu vaccines.

3. Jack fell and hurt his leg. The doctor (take) _____ an X-ray.

4. The baby has an ear infection. The doctor (write) _____

   a prescription for an antibiotic.

5. My husband and I have high cholesterol. We (eat) _____

   less fat. I (buy) _____ more fruits and vegetables.

C **AT WORK** **Pronunciation: Medical specialists** Listen. Mark the stressed syllable. Then, listen again and repeat. 🎧27

súr·geon
car·di·ól·o·gist
oph·thal·mol·o·gist
pe·di·a·tri·cian
fam·i·ly doc·tor

ob·ste·tri·cian
der·ma·tol·o·gist
gy·ne·col·o·gist
al·ler·gist
psy·chi·a·trist

> **CULTURE NOTE**
>
> If a person needs a specialist, his or her family doctor can suggest one. People can also find the name of a specialist by asking their friends or coworkers. What kind of doctor is in each picture on the previous page?

D **ACADEMIC** Talk about Ayumi's day. She has the flu. What is she going to do? What isn't she going to do?

cook	stay in bed
drink a lot of fluids	take a hot shower
go shopping	take a walk
go to work	take aspirin
sleep most of the day	use a heating pad

> She isn't going
> to go to work.

E **LET'S TALK.** Talk with a partner about your plans for today. Write your partner's response and your response to each question.

1. What are you going to do after school?

   is going to _____.
   (Your partner's name)
   I am going to _____.

2. What are you going to do this evening?

   _____.

   _____.

3. When are you going to do your homework?

   _____.

   _____.

4. What time are you going to go to bed?

   _____.

   _____.

Are	you		see the doctor?
Is	he she	going to	stay home from work?
Are	we they		get a flu vaccine?
Is	it		get better soon?

Yes, **I am**.	No, **I'm not**.
Yes, he **is**. Yes, she **is**.	No, he **isn't**. No, she **isn't**.
Yes, we **are**. Yes, they **are**.	No, we **aren't**. No, they **aren't**.
Yes, it **is**.	No, it **isn't**.

A Write the questions and answers. Use the words in parentheses.

1. Mary has a headache. (take some aspirin)

   Is she going to take some aspirin? _____ Yes, ____*she is*____.

2. Joseph has a toothache. (call the dentist)

   _____ Yes, _____.

3. Carol has the flu. (go to work)

   _____ No, _____.

4. I have a sore throat. (you / drink some tea)

   _____ Yes, _____.

5. My brother is in the hospital. (you / visit him)

   _____ Yes, _____.

B **LET'S TALK.** Ask your classmates the questions below. If a student answers "Yes," write the student's name in your notebook. If the student answers "No," ask another student the question. Try to find a student who answers "Yes" to each question.

Are you going to join a gym?	No. (Ask another student!)	Are you going to join a gym?	Yes. (Write the student's name.)

1. join a gym?

2. have a physical examination?

3. get a flu shot?

4. change jobs?

5. move?

6. get a driver's license?

7. get married?

8. visit your native country?

When How Why	am	I		
	are	you		
	is	he she	going to	lose weight?
	are	we they		
When	is	it	going to	get better?

A Discuss the new vocabulary. Then, listen to the conversation between Mr. West and the doctor. Answer the questions. 🎧 28

| broken leg | cast | crutches | ice pack | painkiller | swelling | swollen |

1. What's the matter with Jimmy?

2. Is the doctor looking at the X-rays?

3. What is the nurse putting on Jimmy's leg? Why?

4. How long is Jimmy going to stay in the hospital?

5. When is the doctor going to put a cast on his leg?

6. How long is Jimmy going to be in the cast?

7. What are they going to give him for pain?

B Complete the questions about George. He sprained his ankle while playing basketball.

1. What _is George going to put on his ankle_ ?

   He's going to put an ice pack on his ankle.

2. How long _____?

   He's going to use an ice pack until the swelling goes down.

3. When _____?

   He's going to use a heating pad in two or three days.

4. What _____?

   He's going to take aspirin for pain.

5. _____?

Yes, he's going to use crutches.

6. How long _____?

He's going to use crutches for a week.

7. What _____?

He's going to put a bandage on his ankle during the day.

8. How long _____?

He's going to stay home from work for two days.

C STUDENT TO STUDENT

Student 1: Turn to Appendix C. Read the questions in Set A to Student 2. Student 2 will write the questions in the space below.

Student 2: Listen and write the questions. Then, turn to Appendix C. Read the questions in Set B to Student 1. Student 1 will listen and write the questions in the space below.

1. _____

2. _____

3. _____

4. _____

5. _____

D LET'S TALK. In your notebook, write a conversation between a patient and a friend who is visiting him or her in the hospital. Use the questions in Exercise C. Then, act out your conversation for the class.

> How are you feeling, Marie?

> Well, I feel much better than yesterday.

> How's your back? Are you going to need an operation?

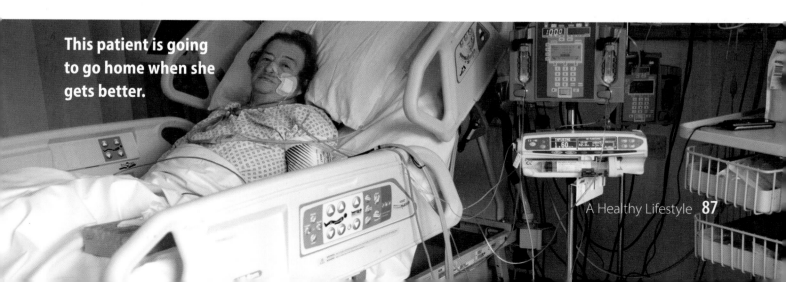

This patient is going to go home when she gets better.

I She They	**will** **won't**	**walk** every day. **join** a health club. **change** jobs.

Use *will* to express an offer to help.
  I'll drive you to school.
Use *will* to make predictions.
  You**'ll** get the job.
  It**'ll** take a long time.

A **Pronunciation: *I'll*** Listen and repeat. 🎧29

1. I'll help you.
2. I'll call her.
3. I'll drive you.
4. I'll make dinner.

5. I'll visit you.
6. I'll take you to the doctor.
7. I'll pick up your prescription.
8. I'll see you tomorrow.

B Read the doctor's advice. Martin went to the doctor with chest pain. Do you think Martin will follow his recommendations?

Change your diet.	Get a pet.	Lose weight.	Start to exercise.	Use less salt.
Cut down on sweets.	Get more sleep.	Lower your cholesterol.	Stop smoking.	Walk to work.

I agree.
I don't agree.

Martin will change his diet.

I don't agree. Martin won't change his diet. He loves fried food.

C Offer to help your friend. She broke her leg and needs help for a few weeks. Use *it, them, him,* or *her* for the underlined words.

1. I can't drive <u>the children</u> to school.
   I'll drive them.
2. I can't make <u>dinner</u>.

3. I can't do <u>the laundry</u>.

4. I can't carry <u>the groceries</u>.

5. I can't answer <u>the door</u>.

6. I can't make <u>the beds</u>.

7. I can't wash <u>my hair</u>.

8. I can't return <u>those library books</u>.

9. I can't clean <u>the kitchen</u>.

10. I can't walk <u>the dog</u>. [Note: Use *him* or *her* in the answer.]

11. I can't change <u>that light bulb</u>.

12. I can't mail <u>these letters</u>.

> I can't drive <u>the children</u> to school.
> I'll drive **them**.
> I can't make <u>dinner</u>.
> I'll make **it**.

D **ACADEMIC** **LET'S TALK.** In groups, make predictions about your class and your school. Then, share your predictions with the class.

The school will build a new cafeteria.

Our teacher won't give us any homework tonight.

All the students will get 100% on the next test.

_____

_____

_____

_____

_____

_____

_____

_____

_____

_____

_____

THE BIG PICTURE / The Accident

A Discuss the new words. Which words do you see in the picture?

blanket	concussion	pale	stretcher
bleeding	confused	pressure bandage	windshield
blood pressure	intersection	stitches	witness

B Look at the picture again and complete each sentence with a word from Exercise A.

1. The man's arm is _____ heavily, so the emergency

   worker is applying a _____.

2. Another emergency worker is taking the man's _____.

3. The woman is lying on a _____.

4. The _____ of the woman's car is broken.

5. A _____ called 911.

C Listen to the story about the accident. 🎧 **30**

D Answer the questions.

1. What are the man's injuries?
2. What are the emergency workers doing?
3. What treatment is the man going to receive at the hospital?
4. What are the woman's injuries?
5. Whose injuries are more serious?
6. What treatment is the woman going to receive at the hospital?

WORD PARTNERSHIPS	
I was in I had	an accident.
It was my fault.	

E Listen again and circle *True, False,* or *NI (Not enough information).* 🎧30

1.	The man went past the stop sign.	True	(False)	NI
2.	The accident was the woman's fault.	True	False	NI
3.	The witness called 911 for emergency help.	True	False	NI
4.	The man has a broken arm.	True	False	NI
5.	The man is going to need stitches in his arm.	True	False	NI
6.	The woman is telling the workers her phone number.	True	False	NI
7.	The woman probably hit her head on her windshield.	True	False	NI
8.	The woman is going to stay in the hospital for a week.	True	False	NI

F Complete the sentences. Use the correct form of *be going to* or the present continuous.

1. The man (lie) _____ is lying _____ by the side of the road.
2. An emergency worker (apply) _____ a pressure bandage.
3. In a few minutes, the workers (take) _____ him to the hospital.
4. The man (need) _____ thirty stitches in his arm.
5. The workers (put) _____ the woman in the ambulance.
6. At the hospital, the doctor (examine) _____ her carefully.
7. A police officer (direct) _____ traffic.
8. He (file) _____ an accident report.

G Listen and write the sentences you hear. Refer to the words in the box for spelling. Your teacher will refer to Appendix D.

insurance	lawyer	overnight	report	stayed	sue

Asthma

Ricky Garcia is going to play outside with his friends. He is taking out his inhaler and taking two puffs. Five minutes later, he's in the park with his friends, running after a soccer ball. Ricky has asthma, but he knows how to control it.

Asthma is a lung disease. The airways of the lungs become **inflamed**—that is, red and swollen—making it difficult to breathe normally. A person with asthma may have wheezing, coughing, a tight feeling in the chest, or shortness of breath. Serious breathing problems are called **asthma attacks**. They can be mild or very serious, requiring immediate medical attention.

Asthma can begin at any age. Childhood asthma, often beginning when a child is younger than ten years old, is one of the most common childhood diseases. Doctors report that the number of young people with asthma is **increasing**. More than six million children in the US have the disease and the number is growing. It is the number-one cause of absence from school. Asthma is often **genetic**. If a parent has asthma, the children are more likely to develop the disease. Children with asthma need to be under a doctor's care. They and their parents can learn to understand this disease and to control it.

It is important to find out what **triggers** asthma. In other words, what causes the attack? The most common triggers are exercise, viral infections, stress, and **irritants** like dust, pollen, or animals. Big cities present added triggers for both children and adults because of air pollution, exhaust from buses and cars, cockroaches, and mold.

There are two kinds of asthma medications—control drugs and quick-relief drugs. Children take control drugs once or twice a day to help prevent asthma attacks. If a child begins to have an asthma attack, he or she needs immediate help, so a **quick-relief** drug is necessary. This medication is often taken through an inhaler. School-aged children usually carry their inhalers with them. This medication works quickly and children begin to breathe more easily in a few minutes. If a child has a serious asthma attack, he may need emergency care at a hospital or doctor's office.

About half of all children **outgrow** asthma, and their asthma attacks stop when they are teenagers. However, many people live with the disease into adulthood. 🎧 31

Air pollution can make asthma symptoms worse.

A Discuss these questions.

  1. Where are your lungs? What do they do?

  2. Does anyone in your family have asthma? What treatment is he or she receiving?

B Circle *True* or *False*.

1.	A child with asthma has breathing problems.	(True)	False
2.	Asthma can begin when a child is two or three years old.	True	False
3.	If a person has asthma, their children will have asthma.	True	False
4.	Air pollution does not trigger asthma.	True	False
5.	Every year, more children have asthma.	True	False
6.	An inhaler can help if a child is having an asthma attack.	True	False
7.	Parents must take the child to the hospital for every asthma attack.	True	False
8.	Many children with asthma need to take medication every day.	True	False

---

READING NOTE

Vocabulary in Context

When you are reading, you will see new words. The meaning, or definition, of a new word is often in the same sentence or in the sentence before or after.

1. The airways of the lungs become **inflamed**—that is, red and swollen.
   Inflamed means red and swollen.

2. Asthma is often **genetic**. If a parent has asthma, the children are more likely to develop the disease.
   Genetic means that a parent can pass a health problem to a child.

C Write the definitions of the words from the article. The definitions are in the same sentences as the words, or in the sentences before or after them.

  1. asthma attack _____ *serious breathing problem* _____

  2. increasing _____

  3. triggers _____

  4. irritants _____

  5. quick-relief _____

  6. outgrow _____

A **ACADEMIC** Take the survey.

Health Questionnaire

1.	Do you smoke?	YES ☐	NO ☐
2.	Do you drive everywhere?	YES ☐	NO ☐
3.	Do you exercise three or more times a week?	YES ☐	NO ☐
4.	Do you eat fresh fruits and vegetables every day?	YES ☐	NO ☐
5.	Do you eat a lot of fried food?	YES ☐	NO ☐
6.	Do you always put salt on your food?	YES ☐	NO ☐
7.	Do you take vitamins?	YES ☐	NO ☐
8.	Do you drink a lot of caffeine?	YES ☐	NO ☐
9.	Do you drink a lot of soda?	YES ☐	NO ☐
10.	Do you eat a lot of sweets?	YES ☐	NO ☐
11.	Do you sleep at least seven hours a night?	YES ☐	NO ☐
12.	Do you drink six or more glasses of water a day?	YES ☐	NO ☐

B Read this text about a student's lifestyle.

In general, my lifestyle is healthy. However, there are a few things **I need to change**.

In the morning, I eat a good breakfast. I always have fruit and then I have cereal or yogurt. For lunch, I order soup or a salad in the small cafeteria at work. For dinner, I usually stir-fry some vegetables and meat and eat that with rice.

But my diet isn't perfect. First, **I love to put** salt on my food. I put soy sauce on everything I cook. I have a salt shaker on my kitchen table, and I add more salt to everything on my plate. From now on, I'm going to buy light soy sauce. Also, I will buy salt-free seasoning and try it. Second, I drink three or four cups of coffee every day. I need a cup of coffee in the morning, but I'm going to **try to drink** decaf in the afternoon and evening.

Unfortunately, I don't exercise enough. I work and go to school, so it's hard to find the time. I like to walk. There's a park near my house. I will try to walk there for thirty minutes on Saturday and Sunday. At school, my classroom is on the third floor. I usually take the elevator, but from now on **I plan to take** the stairs.

WRITING NOTE

Verb + infinitive

Many verbs take the infinitive form. Use an infinitive after *try, need, plan, like,* and *love.*

An infinitive is *to* + the base form of the verb.

There are a few things I <u>need</u> **to change**.

I <u>love</u> **to put** salt on my food.

C Complete each sentence with an infinitive after the verb.

1. I will (try / exercise) _____ try to exercise _____ more.

2. I (plan / walk) _____ to work.

3. I (love / eat) _____ sweets, especially chocolate.

4. I (need / lose) _____ twenty pounds.

5. I will (try / go) _____ to bed earlier.

D Complete the chart. This student organized her ideas before she wrote. She listed three things she wanted to change. Then, she made a plan for each thing.

Things to change	Plans for change
Salt	use light soy sauce, try salt-free seasonings
Coffee	
Exercise	

E Make your own chart on a separate sheet of paper. Write two or three things you would like to change about your lifestyle. Then, make notes about your plans for change. You don't need to write complete sentences.

F Write a few paragraphs about your lifestyle. Then, write about the changes you want to make and your plans for change. Use your chart from Exercise E to guide you.

A **CIVICS** Discuss these questions.

1. Have you ever called 911? Describe the situation.

2. For what kinds of emergencies can you call 911?

CULTURE NOTE

Calling 911

1. Call 9-1-1 for emergencies.

2. Know your location.

3. Stay calm.

4. Answer the questions that the dispatcher asks.

5. Follow the dispatcher's directions.

6. Stay on the phone until the dispatcher tells you to hang up.

These are dispatchers. They contact the police and all emergency personnel directly when a person calls in an emergency.

B Listen to the conversation between a caller and a 911 dispatcher. Answer the questions. 🎧32

1. What is the emergency?

2. Who is calling?

3. What did the dispatcher ask the caller?

4. What directions did the dispatcher give?

C **CIVICS** **LET'S TALK.** Write a conversation between a caller and a 911 dispatcher. Choose one of the situations from Exercise B or C. Then, act out your conversation for the class. You can use some of the sentences and questions from the box below.

What's the emergency?	Is your door unlocked?
Is anyone hurt / injured?	Is the person breathing?
How old is your daughter / father?	Stay on the line.
Where are you?	Stay calm. / Calm down.
What is your location?	The police are on the way.
Are you safe?	Unlock the door.
Are you in any danger?	

AROUND THE WORLD

CIVICS Analyze and compare information about cities and states in the United States

ACADEMIC Compare people and places; scan a text for information; give a presentation

AT WORK Use an online search engine

Landscape Arch in Arches National Park, Utah.

A Write the location under each picture.

One World Trade Center, New York	Atchafalaya Basin, Louisiana	Denali, Alaska
Niagara Falls, New York	~~Mt. Waialeale, Hawaii~~	Interstate 405, California

1. Mt. Waialeale, Hawaii

2. _____

3. _____

4. _____

5. _____

6. _____

B **CIVICS** Read the facts about the United States. Underline the adjectives.

1. Alaska is <u>larger</u> than Texas.

2. Florida receives more visitors than any other state in the United States.

3. The rainiest location in the United States is Mt. Waialeale in Hawaii.

4. Interstate 405 in Los Angeles, California, is the busiest highway in the United States.

5. One World Trade Center in New York City is the tallest building in the United States.

6. Denali is the highest mountain in the United States.

7. Louisiana has more alligators than any other state in the United States.

8. Niagara Falls in New York is one of the most popular tourist attractions in the United States.

9. Atchafalaya Basin in Louisiana is the largest swamp in the United States.

Comparative Adjectives

Type of Adjective	Comparative Form		
One-syllable adjectives	old**er than**	larg**er than**	
Two-syllable adjectives ending in -*y*	bus**ier than**	sun**nier than**	
Two-or-more-syllable adjectives not ending in -*y*	**more** populated **than**	**more** interesting **than**	
Irregular forms	good – **better than**	bad – **worse than**	far – **farther than**

More information in Appendix A.

A Write the adjectives in the correct column.

beautiful	famous	noisy
cold	friendly	safe
expensive	happy	tall

One-syllable adjectives	Two-syllable adjectives ending in -*y*	Two-or-more-syllable adjectives not ending in -*y*
long	busy	populated

B Write the comparative form of each adjective from Exercise A.

One-syllable adjectives	Two-syllable adjectives ending in -*y*	Two-or-more-syllable adjectives not ending in -*y*
longer than	busier than	more populated than

C **Pronunciation: Comparative adjectives** Listen and repeat. 🔊 **33**

1. busier than	**4.** noisier than	**7.** rainier than
2. taller than	**5.** friendlier than	**8.** higher than
3. larger than	**6.** farther than	**9.** sunnier than

D Complete the sentences. Use the comparative form of the adjectives.

1. Florida is (sunny) _____ sunnier than _____ Washington State.

2. New Jersey is (crowded) _____ any other state.

3. Chicago, Illinois, is (busy) _____ Columbus, Ohio.

4. Louisiana is (humid) _____ Nevada.

5. Arizona is (dry) _____ Pennsylvania.

6. Santa Fe, New Mexico, is (old) _____ Orlando, Florida.

7. For surfers, Hawaii is (popular) _____ Maine.

8. New York City is (noisy) _____ Dallas, Texas.

E Circle the adjective that compares your native country and/or city to the United States. Then, work in a group and talk about your answers.

1. My country is **larger / smaller** than the United States.

2. My country is **more populated / less populated** than the United States.

3. The weather in my country is **hotter / colder** than the weather in this city.

4. The city where I was born is **rainier / drier** than this city.

5. The traffic in the city that I come from is **heavier / lighter** than the traffic in this city.

6. The city where I grew up has **more / less** crime than this city.

7. Houses in my country are **more expensive / less expensive** than houses in this city.

8. In my country, gasoline is **more expensive / less expensive** than in the United States.

9. The cost of living in the US is **higher / lower** than in my country.

F ACADEMIC **LET'S TALK.** Work with a partner. Compare yourselves, using the adjectives in the box. Then, tell the class two of your comparisons.

athletic	quiet
busy	short
hair / long	talkative
hair / short	tall
nervous	young

I am quieter than Sofia.

ACTIVE GRAMMAR / *More / Less / Fewer* + Noun

New York Los Angeles	has	**more** **fewer**	universities jobs	**than**	Chicago. Dallas.
		more **less**	traffic noise		

Use *more* and *fewer* with count nouns.
Use *more* and *less* with noncount nouns.

A Describe the differences between a city and a town. Complete the sentences with *more*, *less*, or *fewer*.

1. A city has _____more_____ skyscrapers.

2. There is _____ traffic in a town than a city.

3. Because of the traffic, there is _____ noise in a city.

4. A city offers _____ job opportunities.

5. There are _____ stores and restaurants in a town.

6. There are _____ tourists in a city than a small town.

7. A town has _____ crime than a large city.

8. A town usually has _____ people than a city.

B In your notebook, write two comparative sentences about each fact.

1. Tourists to France: 84.5 million   Tourists to Italy: 50.7 million

   France has more tourists than Italy.

   Italy has fewer tourists than France.

2. Cars in Japan: 60.8 million   Cars in France: 32.3 million

3. Native speakers of Spanish: 389 million   Native speakers of Mandarin: 1.39 billion

4. Saudi Arabia produces 13 percent of the world's oil.   Iran produces 5 percent of the world's oil.

5. Cellphone users in China: 1.3 billion   Cellphone users in India: 998 million

6. People in the US watch 5 hours of TV a day.   People in Canada watch 4.5 hours of TV a day.

Type of Adjective	Superlative Form		
One-syllable adjectives	**the** old**est**	**the** larg**est**	
Two-syllable adjectives ending in -y	**the** bus**iest**	**the** sunn**iest**	
Two-or-more-syllable adjectives not ending in -y	**the most** populated	**the most** interesting	
Irregular forms	good – **the best**	bad – **the worst**	far – **the farthest**

A Write the adjectives in the correct column.

clean	healthy	noisy
fast	hot	popular
friendly	modern	populated

One-syllable adjectives	Two-syllable adjectives ending in -y	Two-or-more-syllable adjectives not ending in -y
high	rainy	expensive

B Write the superlative form of the adjectives in the correct column.

One-syllable adjectives	Two-syllable adjectives ending in -y	Two-or-more-syllable adjectives not ending in -y
the highest	the rainiest	the most expensive

C **Pronunciation: Superlative adjectives** Listen and repeat. 🎧 34

1.	the busiest	**4.**	the noisiest	**7.**	the rainiest
2.	the tallest	**5.**	the friendliest	**8.**	the highest
3.	the largest	**6.**	the farthest	**9.**	the sunniest

D Complete the sentences. Use the superlative form of the adjectives.

1. Alaska is (cold) _____*the coldest*_____ state in the United States.

2. Florida is (popular) _____ state for retired people.

3. (high) _____ city in the world is Wenchaun, China.

4. The Great Pyramid of Giza is one of (famous) _____ structures in the world.

5. Oporto, Portugal, is one of (romantic) _____ cities in the world.

6. The Louvre in Paris is one of (interesting) _____ museums in the world.

7. Ojos del Salado, Chile, is (tall) _____ volcano in the world.

E Match the place and the feature. Then, make a sentence about each place.

Places	Features
___c___ **1.** Greenland	**a.** (large) desert
_____ **2.** Everest	**b.** (cold) place
_____ **3.** The Sahara	**c.** (large) island
_____ **4.** Vatican City	**d.** (long) river
_____ **5.** The Nile	**e.** (high) waterfall
_____ **6.** Antarctica	**f.** (deep) ocean
_____ **7.** The Pacific	**g.** (low) place
_____ **8.** Asia	**h.** (large) continent
_____ **9.** The Dead Sea	**i.** (tall) mountain
_____ **10.** Angel Falls	**j.** (small) country

> Greenland is <u>the largest</u> island in the world.

F In a small group, talk about students in your class. Use the words below.

athletic	funny	organized	serious	tall
friendly	(good) singer	quiet	talkative	young

> Zhen is <u>one of the friendliest</u> students in our class.

> We often use *one of the* _____ to talk about one of a group.

ACTIVE GRAMMAR | as _____ as, not as _____ as

China	is	**as interesting as**	India.
France		**as beautiful as**	Italy.

Colombia	isn't	**as populated as**	Brazil.
Ecuador		**as large as**	Mexico.

Use **as** _____ **as** to show that two people, places, or things are the same.
Use **not as** _____ **as** to show that two people, places, or things are not the same.
  Florida is **not as large as** Texas. = Texas is **larger than** Florida.
  Silver is **not as expensive as** gold. = Gold is **more expensive than** silver.

A Listen and write the sentences you hear. Your teacher will refer to Appendix D.

1. _____

2. _____

3. _____

4. _____

5. _____

B **LET'S TALK.** Give your opinion. Use (*not*) *as* _____ *as* or a comparative adjective.

1. art museums / history museums / interesting

2. Chinese food / Italian food / tasty

3. English / Mandarin Chinese / difficult

4. people in the city / people in the country / friendly

5. a week in New York City / a week in a national park / expensive

> Art museums are not as interesting as history museums.

> I think art museums are more interesting.

Beijing, China

Mumbai, India

ACTIVE GRAMMAR | Contrast: Comparative and Superlative Adjectives

A Complete the sentences. Use the correct form of each adjective.

1. New York is (large) _____the largest_____ city in the United States, but Mexico
    City is (large) _____larger than_____ New York City.

2. At this time, China is (populated) _____ India. By 2025, India will
    probably be (populated) _____ country in the world.

3. Shanghai has (long) _____ subway system in the world, but Beijing has
    (busy) _____ subway system in the world.

4. Coffee is (popular) _____ hot beverage in the United States. In many
    countries, tea is (popular) _____ coffee.

B **LET'S TALK.** In a small group, complete the sentences about
yourself. Then, compare yourself to other students.

> Maria has two brothers and
> five sisters. She has the most
> brothers and sisters.

1. I have _____ brothers and sisters.
2. My house has _____ TVs.
3. I get up at _____ in the morning.
4. I live about _____ miles from school.
5. I can speak _____ languages.
6. I sleep _____ hours a night.

C Discuss these questions. Use adjectives in some of your answers.

1. What is the best soccer team in the world?
2. What is the busiest road in your area?
3. Who is the most famous leader in the world?
4. What is the best movie this year?
5. Which coffee is the tastiest?
6. What is the most interesting place to visit in your area?
7. What is the most difficult language to learn?

> Brazil has the best soccer team
> in the world.

> No way! Italy is better than
> Brazil.

> Spain has the strongest team
> this year.

A Discuss these questions.

1. What is the largest city in your native country?

2. Are cities diverse in your country?

3. Is unemployment high or low in your country?

4. How do most people commute to work?

Los Angeles

B Listen and complete the chart with information you hear about New York City. 🎧 35

	Chicago	Los Angeles	New York
Population	2,704,958	3,976,322	
Percentage of Hispanic origin	29.1%	48.2%	
Unemployment rate	5.2%	5.1%	
Median household income	$50,434	$51,538	
Median home price	$218,000	$605,000	
Average commute time	34.1 minutes	30.1 minutes	
Percentage of people who drive to work	79.1%	72.3%	
Yearly rainfall	36.9 inches	12.9 inches	
Yearly snowfall	36.7 inches	None	
Sunny days per year	189	284	

New York

C **CIVICS** Complete the sentences using the information from the chart in Exercise B.

1. The population of New York is (high) _____higher than_____ the population of Chicago.

2. New York is (populated) _____ city in the United States.

3. Los Angeles has (high) _____ percentage of Hispanics of the three cities.

4. A house in Los Angeles is (expensive) _____ a house in Chicago.

5. A house in Chicago is (expensive) _____ a house in New York.

6. New York has (high) _____ median household income.

7. Workers in New York have (long) _____ commute to work.

8. Chicago has (high) _____ unemployment rate of the three cities.

D **STUDENT TO STUDENT.** Listen and circle the correct city.

Student 1: Turn to Unit 7 in Appendix C. Read the questions in Set A to Student 2.

Student 2: Listen and circle the correct city. Then, turn to Appendix C. Read the questions in Set B to Student 1.

1. Chicago	Los Angeles	New York
2. Chicago	Los Angeles	New York
3. Chicago	Los Angeles	New York
4. Chicago	Los Angeles	New York
5. Chicago	Los Angeles	New York
6. Chicago	Los Angeles	New York
7. Chicago	Los Angeles	New York

Chicago

The Busiest Airports

Three of the busiest airports in the world are in the United States. Los Angeles Airport (LAX) is located in Los Angeles, California. O'Hare Airport (ORD) is in Chicago, Illinois, and Hartsfield Atlanta International Airport (ATL) is in Atlanta, Georgia. These three are the busiest airports in the US because of the large number of passengers that pass through them every year. In addition, these airports move a great deal of cargo (packages, equipment, and so on).

LAX was established in 1928. It is now one of the busiest airports in the world, with 81 passenger and cargo airlines that use the airport. Each year, more than 59 million passengers travel through LAX. About 59,000 employees work at the airport. The employees work at a number of places throughout the airport, including airline counters, coffee shops, bakeries, and the 95 stores where passengers can shop. LAX is a pet-friendly airport with a small pet park where passengers can walk their dogs.

Each year, more than 77 million passengers use O'Hare, another one of the busiest airports in the world, with 70 airlines using its facilities. O'Hare was established in 1945. Today, many frequent fliers know O'Hare because flights often stop in Chicago on the way to other parts of the country or the world. Because so many passengers spend significant time in the airport, O'Hare offers a number of services, such as a hair salon, a children's museum, an athletic club, and a post office. About 52,000 employees operate the airport's 215 restaurants and stores.

Established in 1925, Hartsfield has become the busiest airport in the world. Over 104 million passengers pass through the airport each year. Forty-five passenger and cargo airlines use the airport. More than 63,000 employees work for the airlines and the 263 restaurants and shops. In fact, the airport is the largest employer in Georgia. To help people move from terminal to terminal, or from a terminal to one of the 30,000 parking spaces, the airport has an underground train, which connects all the airport terminals. 🎧 36

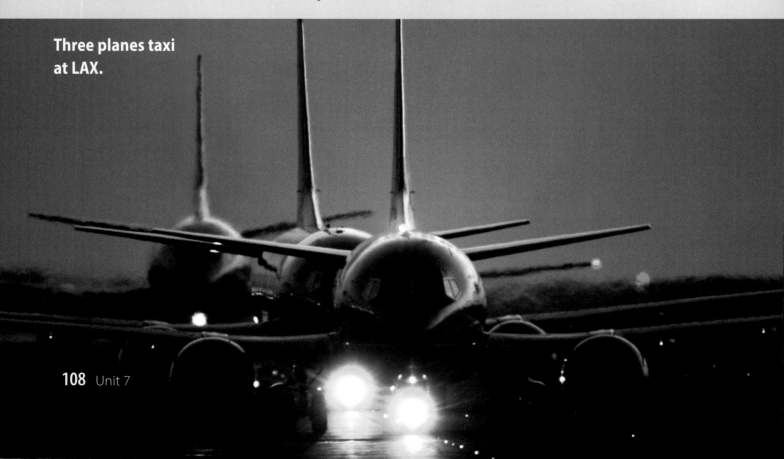

Three planes taxi at LAX.

A Discuss these questions.

1. What is the closest airport to your home?

2. What is the busiest airport in the country where you were born?

3. Do you know anyone who works at an airport? What is that person's job?

READING NOTE

Scanning for Information

When you scan an article, you do not need to read every word. You look through the article quickly to find the information you need.

B **ACADEMIC** Scan the reading and complete the chart.

Airport	Number of passengers	Year established	Number of airlines	Number of employees	Facilities offered
Los Angeles Airport (LAX)	more than 59 million				
O'Hare Airport (ORD)					
Hartsfield Atlanta Airport (ATL)					

C Correct the information. Write the name of the correct airport.

1. ~~LAX~~ ATL is the busiest airport in the world.

2. ORD is the oldest airport of the three.

3. ATL employs the fewest workers of the three airports.

4. ORD is the most pet-friendly airport of the three.

5. LAX handles the most passengers.

6. LAX hires the most employees.

A Read.

Dear Gabriel,

You should come to visit my country, Peru. It is one of the most interesting countries in South America. It has one of the most unusual places—Machu Picchu. Machu Picchu is one of the new Seven Wonders of the World. It is an ancient Inca site, located high in the Andes Mountains. It was the estate of the Inca emperor Pachacuti. You can visit the ruins of over 150 buildings, including houses, temples, and public buildings. One of the most famous places there is the Temple of the Sun. It has wonderful architecture. Don't miss the Temple of the Three Windows. It has a fantastic view of the Andes Mountains.

The best time to visit Peru is from May to September. That is the driest period. The busiest time is around our national holiday, July 28th, so it is better to travel before or after that date. If you come in the wintertime, you can experience one of our most exciting festivals, the Festival of the Sun.

See you in Peru,
Marco

Machu Picchu, Peru.

B Add commas to the sentences where necesssary.

1. Visit Machu Picchu early in the morning late in the day or during the rainy season if you want to avoid heavy crowds.

2. In Peru, the people speak Spanish and Quechua.

3. The Inca people did not use animals iron tools or wheels to build Machu Picchu.

4. Most tourists to Machu Picchu climb a mountain take photos and go back down to the city.

5. Hikers tourists and researchers say that Machu Picchu is a "magical" experience.

> **WRITING NOTE**
>
> Add commas (,) in a list of three or more people, places, or things:
>
> The Amazon, the Nile, and the Yangtze are the three longest rivers in the world.
>
> O'Hare, LAX, and Hartsfield are the three busiest airports in the United States.
>
> O'Hare has many restaurants and stores. (No comma)

C Write a letter to a friend who is planning a vacation. Explain why your native country is a good place to visit. Use some superlatives. Here are some questions you can answer:

- Why should your friend visit your country?
- When is the best time to visit your country?
- What is one of the most popular places to visit? Describe it.
- What is one of the most historic places?
- What is one of the best beaches, lakes, or rivers? Why is it so good?
- What is the most interesting place? Why?
- What is the most fun activity to do in your country?

D Find and correct the adjective mistake in each sentence.

largest
1. Russia is the ~~large~~ country in the world.

2. China is more populated then Russia.

3. The Nile River is more longer than the Yangtze River.

4. The New York subway system is much more longer than the Boston subway system.

5. The Great Wall of China is one of most popular attractions in the world.

6. The most hot inhabited place in the world is Dallol, Ethiopia.

7. California is not as larger as Alaska.

E **ACADEMIC** Give a short presentation to your classmates about an interesting destination in your native country. If possible, bring in a few pictures of the location.

> One of the most interesting places in my country is…

ENGLISH IN ACTION Using an Online Search Engine

A **AT WORK** Discuss these questions.

1. What online search engine do you use?

2. What kinds of information do you look up online?

3. What websites do you often use?

4. Is most information on the internet up to date?

5. How do you know if the information on the internet is true?

WORD PARTNERSHIPS	
look up	a word
	information
	the meaning
	the definition
	the address

Online Search Tips: Keywords

1. Be specific. Put important words first.
   Example: Who won last year's World Series?
   Type: *World Series* + *date*.

2. Use three keywords or more:
   heart disease: too general
   heart disease causes: good—specific keywords

3. Put complete titles and phrases in quotes:
   "Blue Ridge Parkway"

4. Click on *Images*, *Maps*, or *Videos* to get a visual look at the information you want.

B In a group, go online and answer the questions. Write the answers in your notebook. Compare your answers.

URL = Universal Resource Locator, or internet address

1. What is the weather forecast for your city for tomorrow?

2. What is the population of Moscow, Russia?

3. How much is a ticket from the airport nearest you to Honolulu, Hawaii?

4. What are the hours of the Shedd Aquarium in Chicago? How much is an adult ticket?

C Compare your information as a class.

1. Does every group have the same information?

2. Did every group use the same website?

3. Are some websites more reliable than others?

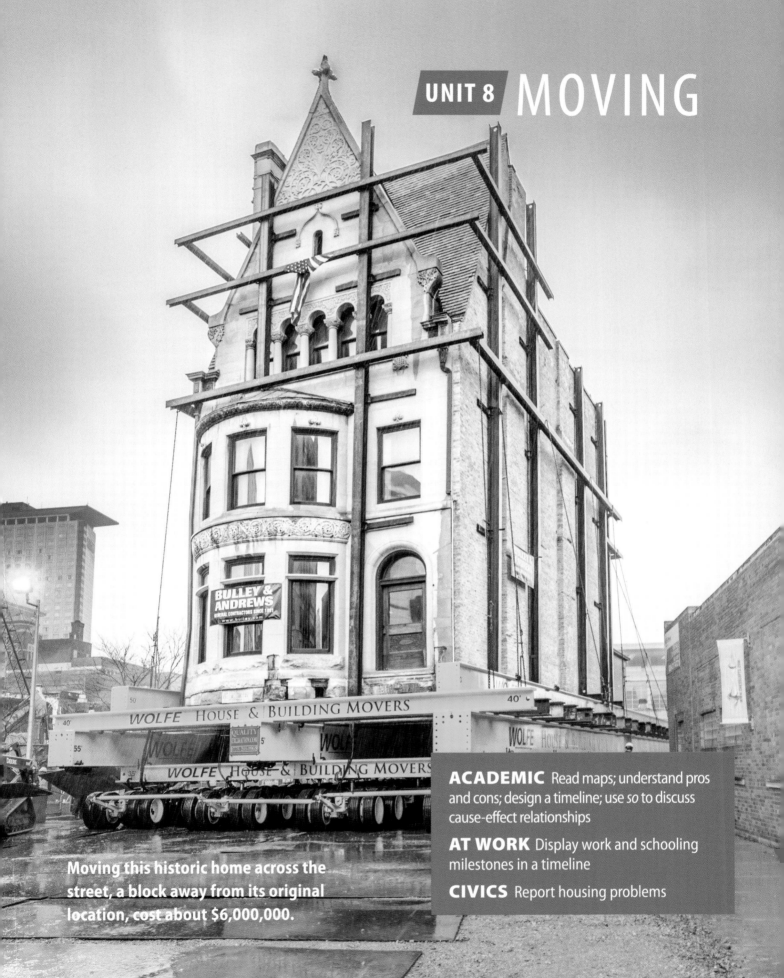

Moving this historic home across the street, a block away from its original location, cost about $6,000,000.

ACADEMIC Read maps; understand pros and cons; design a timeline; use *so* to discuss cause-effect relationships

AT WORK Display work and schooling milestones in a timeline

CIVICS Report housing problems

Some people use units like this one to store their belongings when they move.

A Read and complete.

The average American moves eleven times during his or her life. What is your experience with moving?

1. In my native country, I _____.

   a. never moved **b.** moved once **c.** moved _____ times

2. I came to the United States in _____.

3. I **had / didn't have** family in the United States.

4. Since I came to the United States, I have _____.

   a. never moved **b.** moved once **c.** moved _____ times

5. In the United States, I have lived in _____ and _____.
   (city or state) (city or state)

6. I moved because _____.

7. Now I live in _____. In the future, I would like to live in _____.
   (city or state) (city or state)

8. In the future, I **will / won't** return to my native country to live.

ACTIVE GRAMMAR | Simple Past: Regular Verbs

I	**lived**	in Taiwan.
He	**moved**	to the United States.
They	**signed**	a lease.

1. Regular past verbs end in *-d* or *-ed*. (See Appendix B.)
2. The form is the same for singular and plural subjects.

A Read the story. Write the verbs in the simple past.

Miguel and Ana were unhappy in their last apartment. The apartment had only one bedroom and the kitchen was very small. They (want) _____ wanted _____ an apartment with two bedrooms
1
and a large kitchen. They (look) _____ online and (talk) _____
2 3
to friends. Finally, they found an apartment they (like) _____ . They (sign)
4
_____ a lease and paid a security deposit. Miguel and Ana (prepare)
5
_____ to move. They (pack) _____ their clothes, books, and
6 7
kitchen items into boxes. Miguel (rent) _____ a small truck. On moving day, several
8
of their friends (help) _____ them move. They (carry) _____
9 10
furniture and boxes out of the old apartment and into their new home.

This couple covered their fragile items with paper.

B **Pronunciation: Final -ed** Listen. Write the number of syllables you hear. Then, listen again and repeat. 🎧**37**

> After most consonants, -ed is pronounced as /t/ or /d/.
> After /d/ and /t/, -ed is pronounced /əd/. This adds a syllable to the verb.

1. changed ___1___
2. rented ___2___
3. looked _____
4. needed _____

5. liked _____
6. wanted _____
7. helped _____
8. called _____

9. lived _____
10. painted _____
11. signed _____
12. waited _____

> The final t or d sound is often linked with the first vowel in the next word.

C **Pronunciation: Linking -ed + vowel sound** Listen and repeat. 🎧**38**

1. He lived‿in a small apartment.
2. He looked‿at many apartments.
3. He filled‿out a rental application.

4. He signed‿a lease.
5. He packed‿all his things.
6. He borrowed‿a van.

D Talk about the things Miguel and Ana did when they moved into their new apartment.

1. register their son in school
2. introduce themselves to their neighbors
3. file a change of address form at the post office
4. open a bank account
5. paint the kitchen
6. wash the windows
7. try a few restaurants in town
8. call the phone company
9. change the address on their drivers' licenses
10. apply for library cards

> They registered their son in school.

E Make a list of five things you did before or after you moved. Share your list with a partner.

A Listen and repeat. 🎧39

Base Form	Past	Base Form	Past	Base Form	Past
be	was / were	fly	flew	run	ran
become	became	forget	forgot	say	said
begin	began	get	got	see	saw
bite	bit	give	gave	sell	sold
break	broke	go	went	send	sent
bring	brought	grow	grew	sit	sat
buy	bought	have	had	sleep	slept
come	came	hear	heard	speak	spoke
cost	cost	know	knew	spend	spent
do	did	leave	left	steal	stole
drink	drank	lose	lost	take	took
drive	drove	make	made	teach	taught
eat	ate	meet	met	tell	told
fall	fell	pay	paid	think	thought
feel	felt	put	put	wake	woke
fight	fought	read	read	wear	wore
find	found	ring	rang	write	wrote

B Ask and answer the questions. Use a verb from the list above.

1. When did you come to the United States?
2. How did you come?
3. How much did you pay for your ticket?
4. What did you bring with you?
5. Who met you at the airport?
6. How did you feel?
7. Did you know anyone in the United States?
8. Where did you go when you left the airport?
9. What did you buy your first week in the United States?
10. When did you find your first job?
11. When did you begin to study English?

O'Hare International Airport, Chicago.

ACTIVE GRAMMAR / Past Time Expressions

Yesterday	Last	Ago
yesterday morning	last night	a few minutes ago
yesterday afternoon	last week	an hour ago
yesterday evening	last weekend	a week ago
	last Saturday	two years ago
	last month	
	last year	

Use a time expression at the beginning or the end of a sentence.

A Complete the sentences. Use *yesterday*, *last*, or *ago*.

1. We moved _____ *last* _____ year.

2. My brother visited us _____ month.

3. I graduated from high school six years _____.

4. My sister broke her arm _____ Tuesday.

5. He got his driver's license _____ August.

6. The teacher left the classroom a few minutes _____.

7. I went to the dentist _____ morning.

8. We got married five years _____.

9. I paid my rent _____ afternoon.

10. I came to the United States a year _____.

B Talk about the last time you did the things listed below.

1. buy new sneakers
2. take a vacation
3. come to class late
4. see a movie
5. eat out
6. give someone a present
7. go to a party
8. lose something
9. wake up late
10. get a traffic ticket
11. go to the hospital
12. have a bad cold
13. text a friend
14. drive out of state
15. take a test

I bought a new cellphone last year.

I got a new pair of sunglasses last summer.

I	**didn't live**	in the city.
You	**didn't watch**	the movie.
We	**didn't have**	her car.
She	**didn't lock**	the car.
They	**didn't take**	the bus to school.

Use *didn't* and the base form of the verb to form the negative.

A Complete the sentences about the place where you grew up.

1. I (live) _____ *lived* _____ in the city.

2. I (live) _____ *didn't live* _____ in a small town.

3. I (grow up) _____ on a farm.

4. When I was a child, I (walk) _____ to school.

5. I (have) _____ my own bedroom.

6. We (know) _____ our neighbors.

7. My friends and I (play) _____ outside in our neighborhood.

8. We (lock) _____ our doors.

B **LET'S TALK.** Compare your life now with your life in the country where you grew up.

> In my country, I watched TV two or three hours a day. Now, I'm too busy. I only watch TV on the weekends.

1. watch TV

2. wear a warm coat

3. study English

4. have a cellphone

5. drive

6. eat _____ food

7. go to the market every day

8. work

9. know my neighbors

10. eat at fast-food restaurants

C **ACADEMIC** In your notebook, make a chart. Write three differences between your life now and your life in the country that you come from.

Then	Now
I didn't eat at fast-food restaurants.	I eat at fast-food restaurants once a week.

D Talk about your first year in the United States.

> I arrived at JFK Airport.

> I didn't fly here. I drove across the border at Tijuana.

1. arrive at an airport
2. live with a relative
3. begin to study English
4. like the weather
5. like the food
6. miss my family
7. visit relatives

8. come to the United States with my family
9. find a job
10. call my family a lot
11. meet new friends
12. get a driver's license
13. travel
14. go to high school here

E Listen and complete the timeline about Jarek's life. 🎧 40

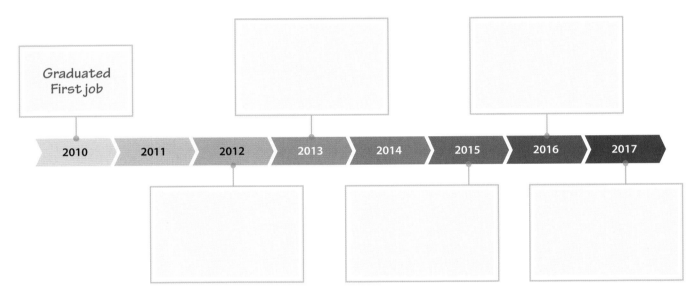

Graduated
First job

2010 2011 2012 2013 2014 2015 2016 2017

F **AT WORK** **LET'S TALK.** Below, draw a timeline with at least seven important dates in your life. Make sure to include work and study activities in the US. Share your timeline with another student. What events did you both include on your timeline? What events are different?

Be	
Present	**Past**
I **am** busy.	I **was** busy.
You **are** lonely.	You **were** lonely.
He **is** friendly.	He **was** friendly.
It **is** safe.	It **was** safe.
We **are** homesick.	We **were** homesick.
They **are** noisy.	They **were** noisy.

1. *Was* and *were* are the past of *be*.
2. The negative forms are *wasn't* and *weren't*.
   I *wasn't* busy.
   You *weren't* lonely.

A Explain the reasons why Boris didn't like his old apartment.

1. neighbors / unfriendly
2. apartment / small
3. appliances / old
4. neighbors / noisy
5. elevator / usually broken
6. neighborhood / (negative) safe

7. apartment / dark
8. rent / high
9. landlord / (negative) helpful
10. apartment / (negative) near public transportation
11. apartment / too far from work
12. basement / often wet

> The neighbors were unfriendly.

B **LET'S TALK.** Complete the conversation with your own ideas. Then, practice it with a partner. Finally, act out your conversation for the class.

A: Why did you move?

B: I didn't like my old apartment!

A: Why not? What was the problem?

B: _____

A: How about your neighbors?

B: _____

A: How much was the rent?

B: _____

A: How do you like your new apartment?

B: I love it! It's _____ and _____.

A Why do people move? Add five more reasons to the list.

1. They get a new job.

2. They want better schools for their children.

3. _____

4. _____

5. _____

6. _____

7. _____

B **ACADEMIC** Listen to the conversation and follow the dialogue on the map. 🎧41

C Listen to the dialogue again. Write the reason for each move in the chart. 🎧41

Move	Reason for move
Puerto Rico to Tampa	*Her father had a job offer in Florida.*
Tampa to Tampa	
Tampa to Largo	
Largo to Tampa	
Undecided	

D Complete the sentences in the simple past. You will use one verb twice. Some of the sentences are negative.

| be   fix   have   ~~live~~   meet   move   rent |

1. We _____lived_____ in the same house for twenty-two years.
2. I _____ Diego a year after we _____ to Florida.
3. We _____ a one-bedroom apartment near my family.
4. The apartment building _____ a lot of problems.
5. The landlord _____ things.
6. One time, we _____ air conditioning for a week.
7. In Largo, we _____ only a few blocks from the beach.

E Listen and write the sentences you hear. Your teacher will refer to Appendix D.

1. _____
2. _____
3. _____
4. _____
5. _____
6. _____
7. _____

F **LET'S TALK.** In a small group, talk about where you live and your future plans.

1. Where do you live?
2. When did you move there?
3. What do you like about your home or area? What don't you like?
4. Do you live near your family?
5. Are you thinking about moving? Where would you move? Why?

Tiny Living

How much space do you need? If you think that you can live in a small, **efficient** space, maybe a tiny home is right for you. Tiny homes are **affordable** alternatives to normal-sized homes. There are tiny house communities from California to Texas to Georgia. The American Tiny House Association can give you more information. There are also TV shows about building tiny homes.

Tiny homes come in many styles. Owners can buy and use construction plans or they can customize their tiny homes. Some homes look very modern, but others look like most other homes—just smaller. One thing that tiny homes have in common is that they are very small, but they have the **essentials**: a place to sleep, a kitchen, a refrigerator, a bathroom, a compact washer/dryer, and an open living space. Others have outdoor space or a balcony. If a person chooses to live in a tiny home, storage space is very important. There is storage everywhere.

There are pros and cons to owning a tiny home. One of the main advantages is the cost. It is cheap to own a tiny home, and the utility bills are lower, especially if the home has solar power. Tiny homes are convenient if an owner decides to move. That is why some tiny homes are on wheels. However, if your home is on wheels, you need a pickup truck to move it. Another advantage is that it takes less time to clean, but you must be organized. A tiny home can be uncomfortable if it is **messy**. Finally, another pro is that a couple will spend more time together. A con is that you will lose some of your privacy.

In Detroit, Michigan, a program is offering tiny homes to low-income single residents. This program helps individuals who have had hard times because of homelessness, prison, or low income. Any person with a **steady** job, even at minimum wage, can apply for a new tiny home. Each home has a kitchen, a bathroom, a living room, a backyard, and a washer-dryer. Some homes have separate bedrooms too. The homes cost between $40,000 and $50,000. The residents pay $1 per square foot, so a home of 250 square feet will cost $250 a month. Similar tiny home communities for low-income residents are available in other states. 🎧 42

This family owns a 238-square-foot tiny home in Pasadena, Maryland.

A After reading, discuss these questions.

1. Do you live in a house? If so, how many bedrooms and baths does it have?
2. Do you think you need more space or less space? Why?
3. Do you like tiny homes?

B Read the statements. Are they *true* or *false*?

1. All of the tiny houses are in California.
2. There are many types of tiny houses.
3. Tiny houses do not have outside space.
4. Tiny houses need good storage spaces.
5. Electricity bills are lower.
6. There is less privacy in a tiny home.

C Match each word with its definition.

___d___ **1.** affordable   **a.** not neat; not in order

_____ **2.** efficient   **b.** very important things

_____ **3.** essentials   **c.** regular; constant

_____ **4.** messy   **d.** a cost that is not too high

_____ **5.** steady   **e.** works with little waste; well organized

READING NOTE
Understanding two sides of an issue Articles often show two different sides of the same issue or idea. These are called the advantages and disadvantages, the pros and cons, or the positives and the negatives.

D **ACADEMIC** Read the article again. List two more pros and cons of tiny homes.

Pros	Cons
1. lower cost	**1.** need a pickup truck to move
2.	**2.**
3.	**3.**

E **▶WATCH** Watch the video and discuss these questions.

1. What are some of the problems with the current housing we have?
2. How do tiny houses help solve those problems?

A Read.

My First Year in the United States

My arrival in the United States was a family affair. My mother and father, four brothers, and I came to the United States from Peru together. My two older brothers met us at the airport. They had been here for many years and they were finally able to sponsor us.

We arrived in October, not able to speak any English. By January, I was studying English at the local adult school.

One of my brothers helped me find a job in a nail polish factory. I didn't like it at all because the salary was very low, and new workers came and went every few weeks. After a year, I was able to attend beauty school and get a manicurist license. When I finished, I got a job at a nail salon. Many of my customers were American, so I was able to become more confident speaking English.

The first summer we were here, my brother taught me how to drive. I passed my driving test on my first try! At first, I only drove near my house, but now I can go a little farther.

I think the first year in a new country is difficult and a little scary, but it's also exciting. It really helps if your family is together and you can help each other.

WRITING NOTE

Using *so*

Use *so* to show the result of an action or a situation.

> I didn't speak English, **so** I couldn't find a good job.
> We didn't like the cold weather, **so** we moved to Arizona.

B Match the two parts of each sentence.

_____b_____ **1.** I didn't like my job,

_____ **2.** My brother already lived here,

_____ **3.** I couldn't speak English,

_____ **4.** English was very difficult,

_____ **5.** Apartments were very expensive,

a. so I came to live with him.

b. so I quit.

c. so I registered for an English class.

d. so I rented one with a friend.

e. so I studied very hard.

C Complete the sentences.

1. I didn't have a car, so _____.

2. My neighborhood wasn't safe, so _____.

D Check the information that is true about your first year in the United States. Complete the sentences.

☐ **1.** I came to the United States alone.

☐ **2.** I came to the United States with my family.

☐ **3.** I found a job at _____.

☐ **4.** I didn't find a job.

☐ **5.** I began to study English.

☐ **6.** I got my driver's license.

☐ **7.** I moved from _____ to _____.

☐ **8.** I traveled to _____.

☐ **9.** I bought a _____.

E **ACADEMIC** Write about your first year in the United States. Write more details about the information you checked in Exercise D. Include one or two sentences with *so*.

F Find and correct the mistakes.

1. I came to ^the United States in 2015.

2. I not have any family in this country.

3. I live with some friends for a month.

4. I found a job, but I no like it.

5. In my country, I have a better job.

6. At first, I am very lonely.

7. I miss my family a lot, so I called them every week.

8. My first year was difficult because I don't speak English.

9. I begin to study English at an adult school.

A   Write the letter of the housing problem under the correct picture.

a. The faucet is leaking.	**d.** The paint is peeling.
b. The lock is broken.	**e.** The air conditioner isn't working.
c. There are cockroaches.	**f.** We don't have any heat.

1. _____

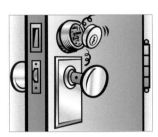

2. _____

3. _____

4. _____

5. _____

6. _____

B   Listen to the conversations. Write the problem and the apartment owner's response.

Conversation 1

Problem: _____

Response: _____

Conversation 2

Problem: _____

Response: _____

> ### CULTURE NOTE
> If you have an apartment, keep a record of your calls with the landlord. Write the date, the time, and the name of the person you spoke to. Keep a copy of any notes you send. If possible, take a photograph of the problem.

C   **LET'S TALK.** With a partner, write a phone conversation between a tenant and a landlord. Then, act out your conversation for the class.

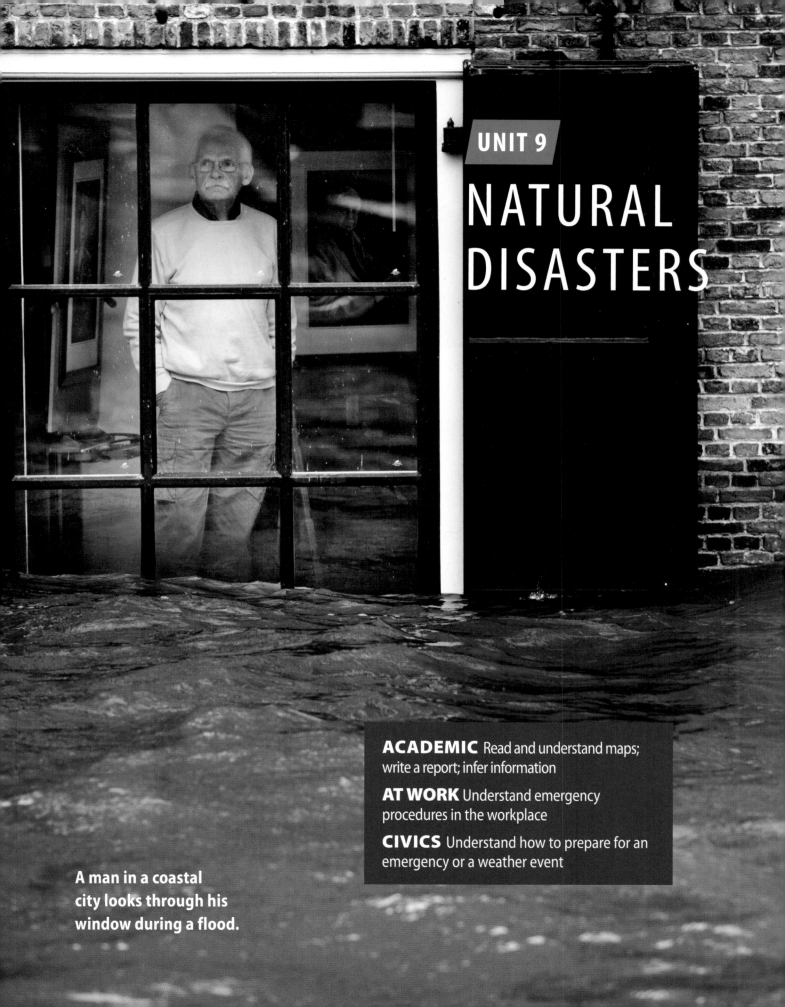

NATURAL DISASTERS

ACADEMIC Read and understand maps; write a report; infer information

AT WORK Understand emergency procedures in the workplace

CIVICS Understand how to prepare for an emergency or a weather event

A man in a coastal city looks through his window during a flood.

A Listen and repeat the words in the box. Then, write the correct natural disaster or event under each picture. 🎧 44

drought	forest fire	snowstorm / blizzard
earthquake	heat wave	tornado
flood	hurricane	volcanic eruption

a. _____

b. _____

c. _____

d. _____

e. _____

f. _____

g. _____

h. _____

i. _____

B Write the letter of the event from Exercise A next to its description.

_____d_____ **1.** We saw a large black cloud in the sky and we ran into the basement.

_____ **2.** The rain was very heavy and the wind was terrible. It knocked down thousands of trees in our area. We lost part of our roof.

_____ **3.** We could see the flames and the smoke for fifty miles.

_____ **4.** The house shook. I quickly got under the table. Some of our pictures fell off the walls.

_____ **5.** The water in the river kept rising and rising. We had to evacuate our house.

_____ **6.** For days before, the mountain made loud noises and smoke came out of the top. Then, there was a terrible explosion and rocks shot up in the air. The lava started to flow down the mountain.

_____ **7.** It was very hot for weeks. The city issued a warning that people should not exercise outdoors. We had our air conditioner on all day.

_____ **8.** It snowed for two days. We had three feet of snow. School closed for three days. It took us two days to shovel our driveway.

_____ **9.** There was no rain all summer. The city declared water restrictions. We couldn't water the lawn or wash our cars.

C **ACADEMIC** Discuss these questions.

1. What is a "natural" disaster? Can you think of any other natural disasters?

2. Have any of these natural disasters ever occurred in your state?

3. Look at a map of the United States. What areas of the United States are more likely to have hurricanes? Snowstorms? Earthquakes? Tornadoes?

4. Which of these events or disasters sometimes occur in your native country?

5. Have you ever experienced a natural disaster? Tell the class about the event.

New plants grow in a forest after a fire.

Were you home?	Yes, I **was**.	No, I **wasn't**.
Was he cold?	Yes, he **was**.	No, he **wasn't**.
Was it windy?	Yes, it **was**.	No, it **wasn't**.
Were they scared?	Yes, they **were**.	No, they **weren't**.

Where were you?	I **was** at home.
Why was she scared?	Because the fire **was** near her house.
Where was the forest fire?	It **was** in California.

A Complete the questions and answers. Then, listen and check your work. 🎧45

1. How deep ___was___ the water? It ___was___ six feet deep.

2. How strong _____ the wind? It _____ a hundred miles per hour.

3. _____ you in Texas during the drought? Yes, I _____.

4. How long _____ the drought? It _____ five months long.

5. _____ there any rain? No, there _____.

6. Where _____ the tornadoes? They _____ in Nebraska.

7. _____ you at home? No, I _____. I _____ in my car.

8. How many tornadoes _____ there? There _____ four.

9. When _____ the earthquake? It _____ last year.

10. How strong _____ the earthquake? Thankfully, it _____ strong.

11. _____ the children in school? Yes, they _____.

12. _____ any children hurt? No, they _____.

13. Where _____ the forest fire? It _____ in the hills near my town.

14. _____ there a lot of snow during the blizzard? Yes, there _____.

15. _____ schools closed for a long time? No, they _____. Schools opened the day after the storm.

Did	you	**evacuate**?	Yes, I **did**.	No, I **didn't**.
	he	**go** to work?	Yes, he **did**.	No, he **didn't**.
	it	**rain** all week?	Yes, it **did**.	No, it **didn't**.
	they	**lose** power?	Yes, they **did**.	No, they **didn't**.

In conversation, *Did you* sounds like /Diju/ or /Didja/.

A **Pronunciation:** *Did you* Listen and repeat. 🎧 46

1. Did you see the tornado?
2. Did you watch the storm on TV?
3. Did you evacuate?
4. Did you have any damage?
5. Did you feel the earthquake?
6. Did you lose power?

B Ask and answer questions about a heat wave. Use the words and pictures below.

Did people exercise outside?

No, they didn't. They exercised at the gym.

1. people / exercise outside
2. people / drink a lot of water
3. the power / go out

4. you / take long, cool showers
5. you / keep your air conditioner on all day
6. you / turn off your air conditioner at night

C In your notebook, write five more questions about the heat wave.

When	**did**	the storm	**begin?**
Where	**did**	you	**stay?**
How many days	**did**	it	**rain?**
How much damage	**did**	you	**have?**

A Write the words in the correct order to make questions.

1. flood / when / the / did / happen / ?
   When did the flood happen?

2. rain / days / how many / it / did / ?
   _____

3. did / evacuate / how many / the city / people / ?
   _____

4. your home / did / have to / leave / you / ?
   _____

5. did / how / your family / get / to a safe place / ?
   _____

6. did / in a shelter / you / how long / stay / ?
   _____

7. have / your home / did / any damage / ?
   _____

B LET'S TALK. Use the questions in Exercise A. In pairs, practice a conversation about a flood. Act out your conversation for the class.

When did the flood happen?   It happened in June.

In August 2017, it rained in Houston, Texas, for four days. Hurricane Harvey brought more than four feet of rain and flooded much of the city.

C **ACADEMIC** Read the article. Then, complete the questions and answers.

A forest fire that burned 15,000 acres was finally brought under control on Wednesday morning. The fire began Sunday in Black Bear Park.

On Monday, the mayor ordered all residents to leave their homes. The police evacuated more than 500 residents. The fire destroyed twenty homes in the area and caused heavy damage to forty others. There were no injuries. Officials estimated the damage to homes and cars at twenty million dollars. The governor declared the town a disaster area.

The fire spread quickly in the hot, dry conditions. It was difficult to fight the fire because of the strong winds.

Police closed Route 40 to traffic on Tuesday because of heavy smoke conditions. Thousands of travelers had to drive an hour north to Route 28 to pass the fire area.

Some residents did not follow the evacuation order. Paul Grayson sent his wife and two children to safety, but he stayed to hose down his roof with water. As flames came near his house, he started thinking, "Am I crazy? Did I stay here too long, just for a house?"

1. How many acres _did the forest fire burn_ _____?
   It burned 15,000 acres.

2. When _____?
   It started on Sunday.

3. Where _____?
   It began in Black Bear Park.

4. How many residents _____?
   The police evacuated more than 500 residents.

5. How many homes _____?
   The fire destroyed twenty homes.

6. How much damage _____?
   There was about twenty million dollars in damage.

7. Why _____?
   It was difficult to fight the fire because of the strong winds.

8. Which road _____?
   The police closed Route 40.

A forest glows in the dark during a wildfire.

D **LET'S TALK.** Work with a group. Write six questions about the snowstorm. Then, join another group. Ask and answer your questions.

A man clears the sidewalk in front of his home after a snowstorm in Boston, Massachusetts.

1. How many inches of snow did Boston get? _____

2. _____

3. _____

4. _____

5. _____

6. _____

E **CIVICS** **LET'S TALK.** Your friends have recently moved to a cold climate. The weather forecast is for three feet of snow! How should they prepare? Write three suggestions.

1. _____

2. _____

3. _____

ACTIVE GRAMMAR / Simple Past: *Who* Questions

Who helped a neighbor after the flood?	Jack **did**.
Who saw the tornado?	Ivan and Raisa **did**.
Who was at home when the earthquake hit?	Ursula **was**.

In these questions, *Who* is the subject.

A Read.

> **Kim and Don** live in southern California. There was a large forest fire near their home.
>
> **Brian** lives in Buffalo, New York. During the last snowstorm, Buffalo got three feet of snow.
>
> **Carla** lives in Kansas. Last week, she saw a tornado coming toward her house.
>
> **Marisa and Marco** live in Florida. They listened to the reports of the hurricane coming toward their city.

B Ask and answer questions about what you read with *Who*.

> Who shoveled the driveway? Brian did.

1. shovel the driveway
2. run down to the basement
3. evacuate
4. have an accident in the snow
5. listen to the weather channel
6. see the fire in the distance
7. hear the tornado warning
8. pack the car and leave

C In a group of five or six students, ask and answer the questions.

1. Who watched the news last night?
2. Who had a big breakfast today?
3. Who listened to the news today?
4. Who listened to the weather report this morning?
5. Who called a family member last night?
6. Who got up late this morning?
7. Who took the bus to school?
8. Who went to bed after midnight last night?

No one did.
I did.
Two of us did.
A couple of us did.
A few of us did.
All of us did.

A **CIVICS** This family is preparing for a hurricane. Explain what they are doing and why.

B Listen to the conversation. Then, answer the questions. 🎧47

1. Where does the couple live?
2. How much warning did they have before the hurricane?
3. What did they put in the garage? Why?
4. What did they buy at the store?
5. Why did they need a power saw?
6. Why do you think they filled the bathtub with water?
7. How strong was the wind?
8. How long was the power out?
9. What damage did their neighbor have?
10. Where did the woman stay during the hurricane?

C Complete the questions with *Did* or *Was*. Then, write the answers.

1. ___Did___ they listen to the weather forecast?   _Yes, they did._

2. _____ there enough warning?   _____

3. _____ they buy water?   _____

4. _____ the wind strong?   _____

5. _____ they evacuate their home?   _____

6. _____ the woman scared?   _____

7. _____ she stay in the bathroom?   _____

8. _____ her husband relaxed?   _____

9. _____ the rain heavy?   _____

10. _____ a tree fall on their house?   _____

D Complete the conversation.

1. **A:** How much warning _did you have_ _____?

   B: We had warnings for about a week.

2. **A:** Where _____?

   B: We put everything in the garage.

3. **A:** What _____?

   B: We bought extra food, batteries, and a power saw.

4. **A:** _____?

   B: No, we didn't evacuate. We stayed in the house.

5. **A:** How strong _____?

   B: It was 80 miles per hour.

6. **A:** _____?

   B: Yes, we lost electricity for two days.

7. **A:** _____?

   B: No, we had very little damage.

8. **A:** _____?

   B: I was so scared! I stayed in the bathroom most of the time.

Tornadoes

A tornado, also called a twister, is a **violent**, spinning cloud that reaches from the **ground** up to storm clouds in the sky. Most tornadoes are weak, lasting only a few minutes, and have winds of less than 110 mph. But the strongest tornadoes can last more than an hour and have wind speeds of 200 mph or more. They can destroy houses in seconds, turn over cars, and pull people, trees, and furniture into the air.

The United States has more tornadoes than any other country in the world. In a typical year, there are 800 to 1,000 tornadoes in the United States. Most **occur** in the middle of the country. Tornadoes **form** when warm and cool air meet. In the Midwest, the warm air from the Gulf of Mexico often meets the cold air from Canada.

Tornadoes can occur at any time of year, but the usual tornado season is from March through May. Tornadoes form most often in the afternoon and early evening. There is often little **warning** of a tornado. People who live in the Midwest know the signs of tornado activity. The sky becomes a dark, often greenish color. Dark clouds appear in the sky and there is often large hail. Suddenly, there is a loud sound, like a train or a jet plane. Sometimes, tornadoes occur in groups. Two, three, five, ten, or more tornadoes can form over a large area.

One of the strongest tornadoes in history hit Joplin, Missouri, on May 22, 2011. Twenty minutes before the tornado, sirens rang, warning of the tornado. Some people heard the warnings, but others did not. The tornado was one mile wide and destroyed everything it touched, including homes, businesses, churches, the hospital, and the high school. The tornado killed 158 people and injured 1,150 others. One family ran down into their basement. Twenty minutes later, when they came up from the basement, nothing was left of their house. At the local Home Depot, the tornado **lifted** off the roof. According to local reports, between twenty-eight and thirty people in the back of the store **survived**, but the eight people in the front of the store were killed.

The safest place to be during a tornado is in a safety shelter, a small underground room that some people build to protect their families. Other safe places are basements or a first-floor bathroom, which is often the most solid room in the house. 🎧 48

This tornado with winds between 166 and 175 mph struck a neighborhood in Katie, Oklahoma.

Analyzing *True* / *False* statements

In a *True* / *False* statement, take note of words like *all*, *every*, *always*, and *never*. These statements are often false. Sentences with words like *many, some, sometimes*, and *often* are usually more accurate.

Look at the difference:

| *All* tornadoes cause damage. | False | *Many* tornadoes cause damage. | True |

A Circle *True* or *False*.

1.	All tornadoes can destroy homes.	True	False
2.	Some tornadoes cause millions of dollars of damage.	True	False
3.	Tornadoes always occur in the afternoon or early evening.	True	False
4.	Tornadoes never occur at night.	True	False
5.	More tornadoes occur in the United States than in any other country.	True	False
6.	All families in the Midwest have safety shelters.	True	False
7.	People always know when a tornado is going to occur.	True	False
8.	Tornadoes can come in groups of two, three, or more.	True	False

B **ACADEMIC** The first word in each line is from the reading. Circle the word with a similar meaning.

1.	violent:	(strong)	dark		**5.**	warning:	typical	sign
2.	ground:	earth	storm		**6.**	lifted:	picked up	destroyed
3.	occur:	happen	area		**7.**	survived:	died	lived
4.	form:	active	develop					

C Complete each sentence with one of the numbered words from Exercise B.

1. A _____ tornado can cause loss of life and property.

2. The tornado destroyed our house, but we all _____.

3. Weather forecasters can predict a hurricane a week or two in advance, but there is often no _____ of a tornado.

4. Tornadoes can _____ at any time of year.

5. The tornado was so strong that it _____ the car off the ground.

D **▶WATCH** Watch the video. Discuss these questions.

1. What are some ways people stay informed during a natural disaster?

2. What important information does the reporter share with the public about this event?

A Look at the notes about Hurricane Katrina. Then, read the report.

Notes:

Formed late August 2005, near the Bahamas

Moved across Florida into the Gulf of Mexico

Became stronger – category 5

Hit Louisiana and Mississippi on August 29th as a category 3

Heavy wind and rain – 8 to 12 inches

New Orleans – very low, below sea level

Strong walls called levees protect the city.

The water went over the levees and flooded the city.

80 percent of city – under water. Destroyed most of city

More than 1,500 people died.

Damage – over $125 billion

More than 150,000 people did not evacuate.

Thousands rescued by boat, helicopter

50 percent of the population left for other cities.

Today – New Orleans – still rebuilding

Damage caused by Hurricane Katrina in New Orleans, Louisiana.

Hurricane Katrina was one of the worst hurricanes in the history of the United States. On August 29, 2005, Katrina hit the city of New Orleans as a category 3 hurricane. New Orleans is located below sea level. Strong walls, called levees, protect the city from water. The water broke the levees and flooded the city. The water flooded 80% of the city. Boats and helicopters rescued thousands of people, but more than 1,500 died. After the storm, more than 50% of the population left the city for other areas. Today, New Orleans is still rebuilding.

A wave reaches Miyako City, Japan, during the 2011 tsunami.

B **ACADEMIC** Write a report about the tsunami that hit Japan in March 2011. Use the notes below. Choose the facts you would like to include.

Notes:

March 11, 2011
Strong earthquake in the Pacific Ocean
This earthquake caused a tsunami.
Tsunami – a giant wave, wall of water
Japan had tsunami warnings.
The tsunami hit northeast Japan.
Waves in Japan: up to 130 feet high
Waves in Hawaii: 11–12 feet high
Waves in California and Oregon: 9 feet high
More than 20,000 people died.

Fires destroyed thousands of homes and businesses.
The Fukushima Daiichi Nuclear plant lost power.
The lost power caused an increase in radioactive material.
The government evacuated residents within 12.5 miles of the plant.
Several countries sent help and financial support to Japan.

C Find and correct the mistakes.

1. There ~~were~~ *was* a lot of rain.
2. There was several tornadoes in Nebraska.
3. Before the hurricane, we listen to the radio.
4. Many people evacuate the city.
5. More than 100,000 people die.
6. The nuclear power plant lose power because of the flooding.
7. The damage to the cities were about 199 billion dollars.

A How much warning do people usually have for these disasters? In a small group, write each disaster in the correct column. Compare your answers with another group's.

earthquake	hurricane	tsunami
flood	snowstorm	volcanic eruption
forest fire	tornado	

WORD PARTNERSHIPS	
issue	a flood warning
	a tornado warning
	an evacuation order

Several Days' Warning	Short Warning	Little or No Warning
snowstorm		

B **CIVICS** Read the emergency directions. Which disaster in Exercise A do they refer to?

1. Secure your home. Move essential items to an upper floor. Turn off utilities. Disconnect electrical appliances. Do not touch electrical equipment if you are wet or standing in water. _____flood_____

2. Evacuate. If there is time, connect garden hoses. Fill any pools, hot tubs, garbage cans, tubs, or other large containers with water. _____

3. Go to a safe area, such as a basement, or to the lowest building level. If there is no basement, go to the center of an interior room on the lowest level (closet, interior hallway) away from corners, windows, doors, and outside walls. Do not open windows. _____

4. Drop to the ground, take cover by getting under a strong table or other piece of furniture, and hold on until the shaking stops. Stay away from glass, windows, outside doors and walls, and anything that could fall, such as lighting fixtures or furniture. _____

C **LET'S TALK.** Work in a small group. There is a forest fire near your home. You have thirty minutes to evacuate. You are not sure your home will be standing when you return. Decide on ten items to pack.

D **AT WORK** Discuss these questions.

1. Do you know what to do in the event of an emergency in your workplace?

2. How are people notified when there is an emergency?

3. Is there an evacuation plan?

4. Have you ever participated in an evacuation drill?

WEDDING PLANS

Friends and family lift the bride and groom while dancing the Hora, a tradition in Jewish weddings.

ACADEMIC Discuss obligations; classify words with similar meanings; write a story

AT WORK Discuss job requirements; describe the application process for a job

CIVICS Identify requirements for a civil marriage; understand etiquette and social rules

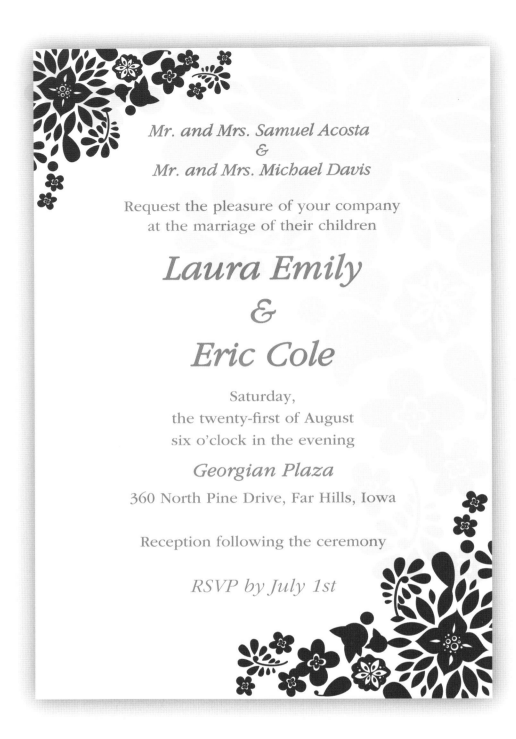

Mr. and Mrs. Samuel Acosta
&
Mr. and Mrs. Michael Davis

Request the pleasure of your company
at the marriage of their children

Laura Emily
&
Eric Cole

Saturday,
the twenty-first of August
six o'clock in the evening

Georgian Plaza
360 North Pine Drive, Far Hills, Iowa

Reception following the ceremony

RSVP by July 1st

A Answer the questions about the wedding invitation.

1. What is the name of the bride? Laura Emily
2. What is the name of the groom?
3. What is the date of the wedding?
4. What time is the wedding?
5. Where is the wedding?

B Work with a group of students—from different countries if possible. Answer the questions about wedding customs in the country where you were born.

1. How old is the average man at marriage? How old is the average woman?
2. How do most couples meet?
3. Do you know any couples who met online?
4. Are marriages ever arranged?
5. Where do most people get married?
6. What do brides wear?
7. What do grooms wear?
8. Who pays for the wedding?
9. How many people usually come to a wedding?
10. What kinds of gifts do people give?
11. Do couples go on a honeymoon after they get married?
12. Does the bride keep her own name, or does she take her husband's name?

WORD PARTNERSHIPS	
get	divorced
	engaged
	married

C Listen to a couple talk about an upcoming wedding. Circle the correct answer. 🎧 49

1. Jack **has to /** ⟨**doesn't have to**⟩ make airline reservations.
2. Travelers **have to / don't have to** buy an airline ticket for a child who is two or older.
3. They **have to / don't have to** make hotel reservations.
4. Jack **has to / doesn't have to** rent a car.
5. Jack **has to / doesn't have to** rent a car seat.
6. Cindy **has to / doesn't have to** find a dress for the wedding.
7. Jack **has to / doesn't have to** buy a pair of black shoes.
8. They **have to / don't have to** remember Calli's favorite blanket.

Skyline of downtown Austin, Texas

I You We They	**have to**	**go** through security. **bring** photo ID.
He She	**has to**	

Have to and *has to* are modals.
They show necessity or obligation.
The base form of a verb is used after the modal.

A Complete the sentences about Jack and Cindy's airport departure. Use *have to* or *has to* and the verb in parentheses.

1. Jack (check in) _____ has to check in _____ online.

2. Jack and Cindy (bring) _____ their driver's licenses.

3. They (arrive) _____ at the airport two hours early.

4. They (check) _____ their large bags.

5. They (wait) _____ in the security line.

6. Jack (take off) _____ his belt.

7. Cindy (take) _____ her laptop out of her bag.

B **Pronunciation:** *Have to / has to* Listen and circle the correct modal. 🎧50

1. (a.) have to   b. has to   4. a. have to   b. has to
2. a. have to   b. has to   5. a. have to   b. has to
3. a. have to   b. has to   6. a. have to   b. has to

C Listen and repeat. 🎧51

1. I have to go to the laundromat.
2. She has to work overtime tomorrow.
3. They have to do their homework.
4. I have to pay my phone bill.
5. He has to get gas on the way home.
6. She has to make a doctor's appointment.

D **ACADEMIC** Discuss with a partner.

1. Name something you have to do before you come to class.
2. Name something teenagers have to do before they can get a driver's license.
3. Name something you have to take with you when you go on vacation.
4. Name something your teacher has to do every day in class.
5. Name something you have to do when you get to work.

> I have to do my homework.

I You We They	**don't**	**have to**	**order** the invitations. **work** today.
He She	**doesn't**		

Don't have to and *doesn't have to* are modals.

They show that an action is not necessary.

A Listen to Hannah's conversation with a coworker. Who does each chore in her family now? Write *D* for *Dad*, *M* for *Mom*, or *H* for *Hannah*. 🎧 **52**

___M___ **1.** clean the house

_____ **2.** clean her room

_____ **3.** cook

_____ **4.** wash the dishes

_____ **5.** do the food shopping

_____ **6.** pay the bills

_____ **7.** pay the cellphone bill

_____ **8.** do the laundry

B With a partner, talk about the things Hannah has to do and doesn't have to do at home.

> Hannah doesn't have to cook dinner. Her father cooks dinner.

C With a partner, talk about your family. What chores do you have to do? What are some chores you do not have to do? How does each person help?

D With a partner, talk about the things that you have to do or don't have to do in your English class.

1. arrive on time

2. buy books

3. bring a dictionary to class

4. attend school in the summer

5. work in groups

6. pay tuition

7. take tests

8. do a lot of homework

9. raise our hands to speak

10. stand up when we speak

11. turn off our cellphones before class

12. write our compositions on a computer

> We have to speak English in class.

> We don't have to study in the library.

ACTIVE GRAMMAR / *Have to / Has to: Yes / No* Questions

Do	I you we they	have to	**work** overtime? **send** a gift?
Does	he she		

Yes, I **do**.	No, I **don't**.
Yes, you **do**.	No, you **don't**.
Yes, we **do**.	No, we **don't**.
Yes, they **do**.	No, they **don't**.
Yes, he **does**.	No, he **doesn't**.
Yes, she **does**.	No, she **doesn't**.

A   **AT WORK**   With a partner, discuss the requirements for your job.

1. What time do you have to check in at work?
2. Do you have to show a photo ID?
3. Do you have to wear a uniform?
4. Do you have to wear any protective gear, or equipment, on your hands, head, or eyes?
5. Do you have to work overtime?
6. Do you have to attend many meetings?
7. Do you have to join a union?
8. Do you have to have special training for your job?
9. Do you have to operate any special equipment?
10. What other requirements are there at your workplace?

B   **CIVICS**   Read the list of requirements for civil marriage ceremonies in San Francisco, California. Then, write a *Yes / No* question about weddings in other countries.

1. Both people have to be 18 years old.

   Do both people have to be 18 years old?

2. The bride and groom have to have legal photo identification.

   _____

3. The couple has to have at least one witness.

   _____

4. The couple has to pay for the marriage license and the ceremony.

   _____

5. Both people can change their last names.

   _____

ACTIVE GRAMMAR | *Had to / Didn't have to*

I You He She We They	**had to** **didn't have to**	**work.** **drive.**

Had to is the past of *have to* and *has to*.
Didn't have to is the past of *don't have to* and *doesn't have to*.

A Complete the sentences about life in the country you come from. Use *had to* or *didn't have to*.

1. I _____ speak English.
2. I _____ work full time.
3. When I lived in my country, I _____ wear winter clothes.
4. I _____ take public transportation.
5. When I was in high school, we _____ do many hours of homework.
6. Students _____ pay for their books.

B Check the things you had to do in your country and the things you have to do now. With a partner, compare your lists.

	Now	Before
Buy car insurance		
Work full time		
Go to the grocery store every day		
Have a credit card		
Be on time for appointments		
Wear winter clothes		
Get a driver's license		
Lock my doors at night		

> In my country, I didn't have to buy car insurance. But here, I have to buy car insurance. It's very expensive!

I You He She We They	**should** **shouldn't**	**get married** in the summer. **send** a gift.

Should is a modal.
Should gives advice or an opinion.

A Complete the sentences. Use *should* or *shouldn't* and the verb in parentheses.

1. Luis and Marta don't have a lot of money. They (have) ___should have___ a small wedding.
   They (take) _____ out a loan to pay for the wedding.

2. I don't think my sister (get) _____ married in the park. What will she do if it rains?

3. If you don't have a lot of money, you (hire) _____ a band.
   You (hire) _____ a DJ.

4. Yolanda and Jim are going to get married in a church. They (choose) _____ a
   reception location near the church.

B **LET'S TALK.** With a group of five or six students, discuss each statement. Then, write the number of
students who agree with the statement and the number of students who disagree with the statement.

	Statement	Agree	Disagree
1.	People should wait until the age of 21 to get married.		
2.	A bride should take her husband's name.		
3.	The bride's family should pay for the wedding.		
4.	The bride should always wear white.		
5.	Money is the best gift to give for a wedding.		

C **LET'S TALK.** In a small group, talk about how to have a long, happy marriage. Make a list of your
five best ideas.

1. _You should go out together once a week._ _____
2. _____
3. _____
4. _____
5. _____
6. _____

D Complete each sentence with a word or phrase from the box. Words or phrases may be used more than once.

~~didn't have to~~	don't have to	has to	should
doesn't have to	had to	have to	shouldn't

Mrs. Sullivan is 40 years old. Three years ago, her husband died, leaving her to raise her two sons alone. Now, her sons are seventeen and fifteen. Before her husband died, she (work) _____*didn't have to work*_____ outside the home. She stayed home and took care of her home
₁
and family. Mrs. Sullivan (make) _____ many lifestyle changes after
₂
her husband died. Now, she (work) _____ full time in order to support
₃
her family. Her company offers good medical benefits, so she (worry) _____
₄
about doctors' bills. Twice a year, Mrs. Sullivan goes away on business, so she (find) _____
₅
someone to watch her children. Mrs. Sullivan is busy, but she is lonely.

Last year, Mrs. Sullivan started to date a very nice widower in her town. He is 10 years older than she is.
He has asked her to marry him. Her sister thinks she (wait) _____ to get married
₆
until her boys are older. Her brother thinks she (look) _____ for a younger man.
₇
But her mother has given her the best advice. "You (listen) _____ to
₈
anyone else. You (follow) _____ your own heart."
₉

E With a partner, read the questions to a wedding planner. Give each person advice. Use *should, shouldn't, have to,* or *don't have to.*

1.
> My fiancée and I want to have a small wedding with our families and closest friends. We can't afford a big wedding. Do we have to invite our bosses?

2.
> I'm getting married in six months. My mother wants me to wear the same wedding dress that she wore, but I don't want to wear it. I want to choose my own dress, but I don't want to hurt her feelings.

3.
> In four months, I'm going to get married for the second time. My first wife and I are divorced, but we are still friends. She's a good mother to our two children. Should I invite her to the wedding?

4.
> I'm the oldest daughter in an Indian family. My parents expect to have three days of celebration and about 300 guests. They would like my fiancé's family to pay half the expenses. My fiancé is an American from a small family. They can't afford to have such a big wedding. I don't want them to feel uncomfortable. What should I do?

CULTURAL NOTE

Some couples have their wedding at a location away from their home. Popular choices for these *destination weddings* are tropical resorts, cruise ships, and other countries. Guests can drive or fly to those locations. Some people join the couple for a weekend, and others stay a few more days—even a week.

A Describe the picture and discuss these questions.

1. What is the agent doing?

2. What is your experience going through airport security lines?

3. Have you ever traveled to attend a wedding? Where was the wedding? How did you travel?

B Discuss the meaning of these words with a partner. Look up the words you don't know.

| veteran | background check | drug screening | metal detector |

C **AT WORK** Listen to the security agent describe his job. Then, answer the questions. 🎧 53

1. When did he become a citizen?

   He became a citizen after he completed his _____military_____ service.

2. How old was he when he got the job?

   He was _____ years old.

3. What kind of examination did he have to pass?

   He had to pass a _____ examination.

4. How long did he wait to get the job?

   He waited for _____.

D Listen again and circle *True* or *False*. 🎧 53

1.	The TSA is a government agency.	(True)	False
2.	He served in the US military.	True	False
3.	He was born in the United States.	True	False
4.	He became an agent six years ago.	True	False
5.	He operates special equipment.	True	False
6.	When he sees something dangerous, he has to tell another agent.	True	False
7.	He sometimes opens passengers' bags.	True	False

E Read the chart about requirements to become a TSA agent. Complete the sentences with *has to / have to / doesn't have to / don't have to* and the verb in parentheses.

Required	Not required
US citizen / US naturalized citizen	Be a veteran
18 years of age	Have previous experience
Pass a background check	Do the same thing every day
Pass a drug screening test	Get a bachelor's degree
Wear a uniform	Like animals

1. Agents (be) _____ have to be _____ citizens.
2. An agent (be) _____ a veteran.
3. All applicants (pass) _____ background checks.
4. An applicant (have) _____ previous experience.
5. Agents (do) _____ the same thing every day.
6. Agents (wear) _____ uniforms.
7. Agents (get) _____ bachelor's degrees.
8. Agents (like) _____ animals.
9. An agent (pass) _____ a drug screening test.

F **AT WORK** The security agent had a long application process. With a partner, discuss your screening for your current job.

1. What forms did you have to complete for your current job?
2. Did you have to have a medical examination for your job?
3. What kinds of screenings did you have to pass?
4. How old did you have to be?
5. Did you have to have any special licenses or training?
6. How long did you have to wait between your job application and your job offer?

It is common for the bride and groom to have photos taken after the ceremony.

Attending a Wedding

You get a wedding invitation from a friend, and you are excited because this is the first American wedding you will attend. Weddings are different from culture to culture. What are the rules of **etiquette** for American wedding guests?

First of all, **respond** to the invitation as soon as possible. The bride and groom have to pay for each guest, so it is important to **notify** them that you will attend. Most wedding invitations include a response card. If you cannot attend, it is **polite** to call the couple if you are close friends.

Read the invitation's envelope carefully. Can you take a guest? Maybe your invitation says, "Marianna Lopez and Guest." That means that you can bring only one guest.

What should you wear to the wedding? Check the invitation for details. For a "black tie" wedding, women wear elegant dresses—called evening gowns—and men wear tuxedos. "Semiformal attire" is usually a dress for women and a suit for men. Remember, female guests should not wear white. The guests should be looking at the bride—not at the other guests.

What rules should you follow at the wedding ceremony? The most important rule is to be on time. You should arrive about fifteen minutes before the wedding begins. If you're late, you should enter quietly and find a seat. If something happens during the ceremony that you do not understand, wait until after the ceremony and ask someone to explain.

> *Please respond by May 30*
>
> M _____
>
> _____ We'd be delighted!
>
> _____ We regretfully decline.

What kind of gift should you buy? Most guests at American weddings do not have to worry about choosing a gift. Many American couples use a wedding gift **registry**. The couple goes to a store or online to register for their gifts. They decide what they need and share their registry information with their guests. The guests look at the registry at the store or online, find out which items are still available, and buy their gift for the couple. Then, the store delivers the gift. You don't have to bring the gift to the ceremony. In fact, it is more convenient if you mail the gift.

Couples also **appreciate** gifts of money. In fact, money is the most popular wedding gift. Place cash or a check in a card that is specially made for money or in a regular greeting card, and put it in an envelope.

Have fun at the wedding! 🎧 54

A After reading, discuss these questions with a partner.

1. Describe the last wedding you attended.
2. How early did you arrive for the ceremony?
3. Did you bring a gift? What was it?
4. What did you wear to the wedding?

etiquette = rules of social behavior

B Circle the correct words.

1. Guests **have to** / **don't have to** respond to the wedding invitation.
2. Guests **have to** / **don't have to** call the couple about the invitation.
3. Guests **should** / **shouldn't** take as many friends as they want.
4. Female guests **should** / **shouldn't** wear white.
5. Guests **have to** / **don't have to** arrive on time.
6. A guest **should** / **shouldn't** find out if the couple registered for gifts.
7. A guest **has to** / **doesn't have to** give money as a gift.

C Match each word to its definition.

___b___ **1.** respond   **a.** a list of gifts

_____ **2.** polite   **b.** to answer

_____ **3.** notify   **c.** to like

_____ **4.** registry   **d.** nice; well-mannered

_____ **5.** appreciate   **e.** to tell

D Discuss the questions with a partner.

1. What are common wedding gifts in the country where you were born?
2. What gifts do most wedding couples in your country appreciate the most?
3. Have you ever attended an American wedding? Compare your experience to the information in the reading.

E **LET'S TALK.** Bring in photos of your wedding or that of a family member. Tell the class about the preparations and the wedding day.

A Read.

An Indian bride displays beautiful henna body art on her hands.

I am from India, and my family arranged my marriage. I was living in the United States when my uncle found a husband for me. My uncle told my father about a man named Justin, who would be a good husband for me. My family and I went back to India for a meeting with Justin and his family. We stayed for about a month. At the end of the visit, I decided to marry Justin. We got married a year and a half later.

The pre-wedding activities, the ceremony, and the reception lasted about a week. On the first day, my family and Justin's family exchanged gifts. During the week, we had to participate in separate religious services. Some services were at my home, and others were at Justin's home. According to custom, the services were only for our families.

The day before the wedding ceremony, my family had to put up a large tent in our yard. About 100 guests attended our wedding. The guests gave us many gifts, including gifts of gold jewelry. We ate sweets and took many photos with our family and guests. The guests also gave Justin and me gifts of money, which his sister attached to his clothes.

On the day of the wedding, a priest married us. The ceremony and the reception lasted about seven hours. After the reception, Justin and I left in a car that his family had decorated with flowers.

Nisha

B ACADEMIC In your notebook, write a story about your wedding or a wedding that you attended. Include the following information:

- Date
- Names of bride and groom
- How the couple met
- Your relationship to the couple
- Country of the wedding
- Location of the ceremony
- Number of people in the wedding party
- Bride and groom's clothing
- Your clothes for the wedding
- Size of the wedding
- Number of guests
- Location of the reception
- Music
- Food

C Read your partner's story. Ask about any details that are missing.

WRITING NOTE

Giving Reasons and Results: *so* and *because*

Because gives a reason:

    1. The couple had a small wedding **because** they wanted to keep costs down.

    2. The groom didn't have to rent a tuxedo **because** he decided to wear his best suit.

So gives a result:

    3. The couple wanted to keep costs down, **so** they had a small wedding.

    4. The groom decided to wear his best suit, **so** he didn't have to rent a tuxedo.

D Complete with *because* or *so*.

    1. The bride's sister works at a bakery, _____*so*_____ they don't have to buy a cake.

    2. The groom doesn't own a suit, _____ he is going to rent one.

    3. The bride and groom are taking dance classes _____ they aren't good dancers.

    4. The bride and groom are saving money _____ they want to go to Europe on their honeymoon.

    5. The bride can't find a dress that she likes, _____ she's going to go to a dressmaker for something special.

    6. The bride and groom are going to two florists today _____ they want to choose the flowers for the reception.

A **CIVICS** Discuss these customs in the United States. Is each custom the same or different in the country where you were born?

1.

Women sometimes hug or kiss a friend once on the cheek when they meet.

2.

Men often shake hands or give a friend a pat on the back when they meet.

3.

People stand a comfortable distance apart when they speak.

4.

People stand in line at buses, stores, and ticket counters. It is not polite to push or cut in line.

B In a group, talk about customs in your country and in the United States.

1. When you enter a house, do you remove your shoes?
2. What time do people arrive for meetings and appointments?
3. If you are invited to dinner, do you bring a gift for the host?
4. If you are invited to a party that begins at 9:00, what time do you arrive?
5. What US custom do you find very different from your country?

AT WORK Match a job with its required skills; describe a job; read and understand signs in the workplace; discuss workplace policies and regulations; describe a work style; prepare for a job interview

ACADEMIC Make a polite request; make predictions; edit a piece of writing

CIVICS Discuss general regulations; understand classroom rules

A fisherman carries his catch of lobsters.

A Look at the photos and write the jobs.

1. _____ 2. _____ 3. _____

B Match each occupation with the job skill.

> *Can* is a modal.
> It shows ability.

_c_ **1.** hairdresser   **a.** I can plan roads, bridges, and tunnels.

_____ **2.** optometrist   **b.** I can help you file your income taxes.

_____ **3.** civil engineer   **c.** I can cut and color hair.

_____ **4.** health aide   **d.** I can check your eyes and prescribe glasses or contacts.

_____ **5.** accountant   **e.** I can take a pulse and blood pressure.

_____ **6.** mechanic   **f.** I can give a car a tune-up.

_____ **7.** florist   **g.** I can help you with car, house, and life insurance.

_____ **8.** insurance agent   **h.** I can arrange flowers for weddings.

C **AT WORK** Describe a job. Use *can*. Your classmates will guess what the job is.

> I can make furniture.

> Are you a carpenter?

> Yes, I am.

A carpenter builds furniture in his shop.

ACTIVE GRAMMAR / *Could you / Would you*

Could you please	call Mr. Henderson?
Would you please	copy this report?

> *Could* and *would* are modals.
> Use *could you* and *would you* to make polite requests.
> Could you please copy this report?

A | **ACADEMIC** | Restate each sentence as a polite request.

1. Fill out this form.
   Could you please fill out this form?
2. Take this call.
3. Send an email to the employees.
4. Clean the workroom.
5. Fill this order.
6. Take Ms. Miller's temperature.
7. Bring me some change.
8. Open the door for me.
9. Help the next customer.
10. Unpack those boxes.

B Listen. Then, write the request for each item. 🎧55

1.

   Could you please answer the phone?

2.

   _____

3.

   _____

4.

   _____

C **Pronunciation:** *Would you* **and** *Could you* Listen again. Repeat each request in Exercise B. 🎧55

D In your notebook, write three more requests.

Student-to-student requests: Could I please use your dictionary?

Teacher-to-student requests: Would you please hand in your papers?

ACTIVE GRAMMAR / *Must / Must not / Can't*

I You He	**must**	**wear** a name tag. **sign** in. **file** a report.

I You He	**must not** **can't**	**make** personal calls. **argue** with a customer. **use** a cellphone.

Must, must not, and *can't* are modals.
Must states rules, policies, and regulations.
Can't and *must not* show that an action is not allowed or not permitted.

A **AT WORK** Explain what each work sign means. Use *must, must not,* or *can't.*

1.

You must wear a hard hat.

2.

3.

4.

5.

6.

7.

8.

9.

10.

11.

12.

B LET'S TALK. Work in a small group. Write four of your school or class rules.

Students must not copy from other students during an exam.

You must turn off your phone during class.

_____

_____

_____

_____

C AT WORK Talk about these company policies and regulations. Use *must*, *must not*, or *can't*.

1. Work hours: 8:00–4:00.
2. Punch in and out.
3. If you are late, call your supervisor.
4. Wear your ID tag at all times.
5. No jeans or athletic clothing.
6. No smoking.

7. No cellphones.
8. Do not bring your children to work.
9. Report unsafe working conditions.
10. No offensive pictures on office walls.
11. Report any accidents immediately.
12. Use the internet for business only.

> Workers must report to work by 8:00.

D CIVICS With a partner, discuss these questions.

1. What are some rules at your workplace?
2. What are some regulations at an airport?
3. What are some laws about children in cars?
4. What are some laws about texting and using cellphones while driving?
5. What are some laws about pets?
6. What are some common apartment regulations?

WORD PARTNERSHIPS	
clock	in
sign	
punch	out
swipe my card	

This welder must wear a welding mask to protect his face.

I He They	**may (not)** **might (not)**	**change** jobs. **get** a promotion. **take** a sick day.

May and *might* are modals.
May and *might* show possibility.

A Complete the sentences. Write what may or might happen.

1. Yolanda got to work late today, so the boss _____ *might give her a warning* _____.

2. You need a job. A new clothing store is opening in your area, so you
   _____.

3. Nelson has a bad cold. He _____ to work.

4. The boss is very happy with Mia's work. He _____.

5. The economy is bad and our company is not doing very well. The boss
   _____.

6. The economy is very good and our company is doing very well. The boss
   _____.

7. Shelly works full time. She wants to begin college in the fall. She _____
   her job in the fall.

B **ACADEMIC** Talk about the pictures with a partner. Then, in your notebook, write two sentences about what may or might happen in each.

> She might slip on the floor.

1.

2.

3.

4.

5.

6.

ACTIVE GRAMMAR / *May* and *Might* vs. Future

I **might go** to nursing school. **Maybe** I **will go** to nursing school. I**'m going to go** to nursing school. I **will go** to nursing school.	*May* and *might* are modals. They show possibility. *Maybe* also shows possibility. *Maybe* is the first word in a sentence. *Will* and *(be) going to* show that you are sure or certain.

A Rewrite the sentences. Use *may* or *might*.

1. Maybe I will quit my job. _____ I may / might quit my job. _____

2. Maybe the boss is going to fire him. _____

3. Maybe she will get the job. _____

4. Maybe we are going to have a test. _____

B In a small group, talk about your future plans. Use *may*, *might*, *maybe*, or the future.

I might change jobs.

Maybe I will change jobs.

I don't like my job. I will change jobs soon.

1. change jobs
2. get a dog
3. visit my native country
4. open a small business
5. continue to study English
6. take a computer class
7. take out a loan
8. go on a cruise
9. buy a new TV
10. move
11. paint my bedroom
12. visit friends

C With a partner, ask and answer the questions. Use *may*, *might*, or the future.

1. What are you going to have for dinner tonight?
2. What are you going to do this weekend?
3. Where are you going to go on your next vacation?
4. When are you going to have a party?
5. When are you going to go to the dentist?

Modal	Meaning	Example
have to	obligation necessity	I **have to do** my homework.
(not) have to	no obligation no necessity	I **don't have to get up** early on Sunday.
should	advice opinion	You **should apply** for the job. You **should wear** a suit.
must	necessity a rule or policy	I **must pay** taxes.
must not can't	something is not permitted	I **must not park** here. I **can't wear** jeans to work.
can	ability	I **can fix** a flat tire.
could would	polite request	**Could** you **answer** the phone? **Would** you **file** these papers?
may might	possibility	I **may get** the job. I **might lose** my job.

NOTE: Modals change the meaning of a verb.

After a modal, use the base form of the verb. Do not use -s, -ed, or -ing.

A Circle the correct modal.

1. Tony has a job interview. He **should** / **doesn't have to** arrive on time.
2. At our company, all employees **must / might** wear name tags.
3. A nurse **has to / must not** wash her hands after caring for each patient.
4. Work begins at 7:30. You **must not / don't have to** arrive late.
5. **Could you / Should you** please repair the copy machine?
6. You are very good at math. I think you **should / have to** study accounting.
7. Friday is casual dress day. We **have to / don't have to** wear suits.
8. I received a good evaluation, so I **have to / might** get a raise.
9. Employees **must not / don't have to** take home company products.
10. You aren't happy at your job. You **should / have to** look for another opportunity.
11. We **don't have to / can't** make personal phone calls at work.

B Listen. Circle the letter of the sentence with the same meaning as the sentence you hear. 🎧56

1. **a.** I should take a break.
   b. I might take a break.

2. **a.** Could you please look up the number?
   b. You should look up the number.

3. **a.** You don't have to smoke.
   b. You must not smoke.

4. **a.** You might get a haircut.
   b. You should get a haircut.

5. **a.** You must renew your license.
   b. You might renew your license.

6. **a.** We don't have to work.
   b. We must not work.

C **AT WORK** Complete the conversations. Stephan is asking questions about his new workplace. Use a modal and the verb in parentheses.

1. **A:** What time does work begin?

   B: All employees (sign in) _____ *have to / must sign in* _____ by 8:00.

2. **A:** Which office will I work in?

   B: We're not sure yet. You (be) _____ in Room 245. Or you
   (be) _____ in Room 246. We're going to decide later today.

3. **A:** What papers do I need to fill out?

   B: You (complete) _____ your tax withholding form and
   an employee data form.

4. **A:** What is the dress code here?

   B: It's pretty casual—nice pants and a sweater are fine. You (wear) _____
   a suit. But don't dress too casually. You (wear) _____ jeans and a T-shirt.

D **CIVICS** Talk about your classroom rules. Use modals. [We don't have to stand up when we speak.]

1. stand up when we speak
2. do our homework
3. speak English in class
4. bring coffee into our classroom
5. pay for our books
6. have a fire drill this month
7. turn off our cellphones
8. call our teacher by their first name
9. wear jeans to class
10. have a test next week

E **LET'S TALK.** With a partner, write three sentences about your class. Use modals. Then, read your sentences to the class. Your classmates will decide if the sentences are true or false.

A Discuss these questions.

1. What kinds of tests does a diagnostic medical lab perform?
2. Who are some of the employees at a diagnostic lab?
3. What kind of paperwork does a medical lab keep?

> A diagnostic medical lab performs medical tests ordered by a doctor.

B Listen and look at the pictures. Sharon Taylor is an administrative assistant in a diagnostic lab. Write six of her responsibilities. 🎧 57

1. _She schedules employees._

2. _____

3. _____

4. _____

5. _____

6. _____

C Complete the sentences. Use the correct modal and the verb in parentheses. In some sentences, more than one answer is correct.

1. (work) _____*Could you please work*_____ an extra hour today? Carla needs to leave early.

2. If you want a copy of your lab results, you (call) _____ this number.

3. The lab sends the test results to the doctor. The patient (bring) _____ the results to the doctor.

4. (add) _____ two boxes of latex gloves to our order?

5. For a fasting blood test, a patient (eat or drink) _____ anything for twelve hours.

6. (make) _____ a copy of this insurance card?

7. If a patient has insurance, he (bring) _____ his insurance card.

8. If a patient has insurance, she (pay) _____ the full amount.

9. If a patient doesn't have insurance, he (pay) _____ for the test.

D **AT WORK** Discuss the qualities of a good employee in the box. Then, complete the sentences.

confident
good with details
patient
team player
well-organized
~~works well under pressure~~

1. The office is always busy, but Sharon _____*works well under pressure*_____.

2. Sharon sometimes needs to repeat information, but she is always _____.

3. Everyone knows the responsibilities and schedule, so it is a _____ office.

4. Sharon knows how to run the office. She feels _____ in her abilities.

5. Sharon manages all the supplies and orders. She's _____.

6. Sharon works well with others. She is a good _____.

E Think about your work style. Circle *Yes* or *No* for each statement. Then, talk about your answers in a group.

1. I'm always patient with customers or clients.   Yes   No
2. I am a good team player.   Yes   No
3. I work well under pressure.   Yes   No
4. I am organized and good with details.   Yes   No
5. I feel confident at my job.   Yes   No

READING NOTE

A Humorous Article

Sometimes an article is not serious. It looks at a situation from a comical or funny point of view. For example, this article explains what you should *never* do at work.

How to Lose Your Job in Five Easy Steps

1. Don't worry about time policies.

If you have a half hour for lunch, no one is going to say anything if you take an extra ten minutes. If work begins at 8:30, arrive at 8:45. You can always **blame** the heavy traffic. No one is counting how many breaks you take. If you have two breaks, no one will **notice** if you take three.

2. Blame your coworkers if you miss a deadline or do a poor job on a project.

Be sure that nothing is your **fault**. If the boss complains about your work, explain to him that "Randy gave me the wrong directions." Or say, "I did my part. Tom didn't do his part."

3. Don't worry about the office dress code.

You should wear what you like to work. Be comfortable. You don't need to wear the **traditional** dress style of the older employees. Shorts, sweatpants, and T-shirts are always appropriate.

4. Post your feelings about work online.

You can **trust** all your friends. No one will share your posts. Your boss and your company don't follow what is happening online. They will never see posts like these:

"My boss always **complains** about everyone. But no one ever sees *him* working."

"I lied to my boss today. I told her I had a big exam and needed the day off. Hah! She believes anything!"

5. Call other employees by nicknames.

Give each employee a funny name based on their personality or their habits. If a coworker eats candy all the time, call him *Jelly Beans*. He'll think it's funny. 🎧58

A chair race at the office.

A **AT WORK** After reading, discuss these questions.

1. What time does your work begin? What is the policy about arriving late?
2. What is the dress code at your work place?
3. Who speaks to an employee who does not follow a policy?

B Discuss the meaning of the words in the box. Then, write the letter of the correct answer.

blame	complain	fault	notice	traditional	trust

1. Jorge often complains about ___a___.
   a. his schedule   b. the internet
2. The accident was his fault. He _____ at the red light.
   a. stopped   b. didn't stop
3. The boss noticed that one of the employees _____.
   a. was wearing a uniform   b. was leaving early
4. The boss blamed the secretary for _____ the copy machine.
   a. breaking   b. fixing
5. The boss trusted the team to _____.
   a. complete the project   b. make a mistake
6. Employees should wear traditional clothes, such as _____.
   a. jeans and a T-shirt   b. nice pants and a button-down shirt

C Change the suggestions. How can you *keep* your job?

1. If work begins at 8:30, arrive at 8:45.
   If work begins at 8:30, arrive at 8:20.

2. Blame your coworkers if you do a poor job on a project.

3. Wear shorts, sweatpants, and T-shirts to work.

4. Post your feelings about work online.

5. Take an extra break.

6. It's fine to give nicknames to other employees.

A **AT WORK** Discuss these questions. Then, read Tony's story.

1. Where do you work?
2. What do you do there?
3. What do you like about your job? What don't you like?

A carpet specialist.

I work for A1 Carpet Cleaning in Amesville. My company cleans rugs and carpets, and strips and waxes floors. I'm a carpet specialist. On most days, I clean carpets in four different homes. We work in teams—there are always two people together because there is a lot of equipment to carry into the house. First, we put small floor protectors under all furniture legs. Next, we remove any stains in the carpet. Then, we lightly shampoo the carpet and remove the water, both with the same machine.

I work the day shift, from 8:00 to 4:00. We have to wear company uniforms. Everyone must wear an ID at all times. When I arrive at work, my boss gives me the names, addresses, and phone numbers of the homes I have to visit that day. I drive a small company truck and I have to be very careful. If I have an accident, I might lose my job. When I arrive at a home, I have to call the office. When I finish the job, I have to call the office again.

I like my boss because she is organized and helpful. I also like my hours. I'm home by 5:00, and I don't have to work on the weekends. I get two weeks' paid vacation every year. There is one major problem with my job, though. I don't have any health benefits.

Adding Details
Details make a story more interesting. Give specific information and examples when you write.

B Read the text below. The writer did not give many details. What questions can you answer?

> I work for a carpet cleaning company. I'm a carpet specialist. I clean carpets in homes.
>
> I work the day shift. We have to wear a white company shirt. When I arrive at work, my boss tells me the houses I have to visit that day.
>
> I like my boss. I also like my hours. I get two weeks' paid vacation every year. I don't have any health benefits.
>
> Martin

1. What is the company's name? What town is it in? *We don't know.*

2. Does Martin work alone?

3. What does he do when he gets to a house?

4. What are his hours?

5. What does he wear?

6. What are some of the company policies and procedures?

7. Why does he like the boss?

8. Does this composition have many details?

9. Which composition is more interesting, the one on the previous page or this one?

C Write a few notes about your job or a job you would like to have. Then, write a few paragraphs about the job. Include a lot of details.

Company and location	
Job title	
Job responsibilities	
Hours	
Uniform or dress code	
Policies	
Things I like	
Things I don't like	

D In a small group, read your stories to one another. Ask questions about the jobs.

E **ACADEMIC** Revise your work. Add the information that your classmates asked about.

A Read the interview tips.

Interview Tips

1. Research the company.
2. Practice the interview several times.
3. Dress appropriately.
4. Arrive a few minutes early for the interview. Turn off your cellphone!
5. Shake hands with the interviewer.
6. Look at the interviewer. Make eye contact. Smile from time to time.

7. Explain your strengths. Talk about your skills.
8. Answer questions clearly. Give a few details in each answer.
9. Thank the interviewer and shake hands again.
10. Send a thank-you note two or three days after the interview.

B **AT WORK** In a group, ask and answer the interview questions about a job you would like.

1. What are your job responsibilities now?
2. What skills do you have?
3. Why do you want to work for us?
4. What are your strengths?
5. Why should we hire you?
6. What questions do you have for us?

C **LET'S TALK.** With a partner, practice an interview for a manager position. Then, two or three pairs will role-play their interviews for the class. Look at the interview tips. What did the job applicant do well? How can the applicant improve his or her interview skills?

D Look at the picture. The people are waiting for job interviews. How can they improve their chances of getting a job? Use *should* or *shouldn't*.

WORKING PARENTS

A member of the European Parliament with her daughter during a work session.

765

ACADEMIC Understand a sequence of events; match phrasal verbs and their meanings

AT WORK Read about working parents

CIVICS Write a note to a teacher; read a report card; learn about before- and after-school care

A Look at the pictures and listen to Henry's schedule. 🎧 59

1.

2.

3.

4.

5.

6.

B **Pronunciation: Pauses** Listen and repeat. Pay attention to the pause at the comma. 🎧 60

1. After he drops off the children, Henry stops at a coffee shop.
2. As soon as the children get home from school, they call their father.
3. After they eat dinner, Henry helps the children with their homework.
4. When they finish their homework, they can play video games.
5. Before he goes to sleep, Henry watches TV.

He watches TV **before** <u>he goes to bed</u>. **Before** <u>he goes to bed</u>, he watches TV.
(main clause)   (time clause)   (time clause)   (main clause)

1. A time clause explains when an action happens. It begins with a word such as *after*, *before*, *when*, *as soon as*, *until*, or *if*. A time clause has a subject and a verb.

2. If the time clause is at the beginning of the sentence, use a comma after the time clause. If the time clause is at the end of the sentence, don't use a comma.

> **As soon as** Henry gets home, he asks the children about school.
> The children play games **until** their father comes home.

A **ACADEMIC** Circle *True* or *False*.

1.	After Henry gets to work, he drops off the children at school.	True	False
2.	Before he drops off the children, Henry gets a cup of coffee.	True	False
3.	As soon as the children get home, they call their father.	True	False
4.	As soon as the children get home, Henry leaves work.	True	False
5.	The children eat dinner before Henry gets home from work.	True	False
6.	After the children do their homework, they can play video games.	True	False
7.	Henry watches TV after the children go to bed.	True	False

B Listen to Henry's conversation with his coworker, Mark. Then, practice it with a partner. 🎧61

Mark: You get a call every day at 3:15, don't you?

Henry: Yes, that's my son. He's 11. My daughter is 10. They walk home together after school. My son has to call me as soon as they walk in the door.

Mark: Oh, I see. My boys are still little. They stay at daycare until I pick them up at 4:30.

Henry: Big kids, little kids. . . Childcare is a challenge when you're working.

A father takes his baby to daycare on his way to work.

C Underline the time clauses.

1. Tammy stays in bed until she hears Emma wake up.

2. As soon as Emma wakes up, she wants her bottle.

3. After Emma has her bottle, Tammy feeds her breakfast.

4. Emma has breakfast before Tammy gets her dressed.

5. While Emma plays in her crib, Tammy takes a shower and gets dressed.

D Listen to Tammy talk about Emma's day. Take notes. 🎧 62

7:00 ___bottle, breakfast___   4:00 _____

9:00 _____   5:00 _____

10:30 _____   6:00 _____

12:00 _____   7:00 _____

1:00 _____   8:00 _____

E Complete the sentences. Use *before*, *after*, *when*, *as soon as*, or *until*.

1. Tammy is going to stay home ___until___ Emma is two years old.

2. _____ Emma wakes up, she has a bottle.

3. _____ she has her bottle, she eats breakfast.

4. Tammy cleans the house _____ she takes Emma to the park.

5. They stay at the park _____ it is time for lunch.

6. Emma takes a nap _____ she eats lunch.

7. _____ Tammy takes Emma to the library, she checks out five or six books.

8. Emma plays with her father _____ they eat dinner.

9. Her father reads her a story _____ she goes to bed.

F Combine the sentences using the time words. First, write the sentence with the time clause at the beginning of the sentence. Then, write the sentence with the time clause at the end.

1. I turn on my computer. I check my email. (after)

   After I turn on my computer, I check my email.

   I check my email after I turn on my computer.

2. He gets up. He has a cup of coffee. (as soon as)

   _____

   _____

3. I leave for school. I make my bed. (before)

   _____

   _____

4. She gets to school. She talks with her friends. (when)

   _____

   _____

5. I am busy every moment. I go to sleep at night. (until)

   _____

   _____

G **LET'S TALK.** Write your daily schedule in the chart. Then, tell a partner about your day. Give more details as you talk. Use *before*, *after*, *as soon as*, and *when* in your description.

Time	Activity
	turn off the alarm
	go to sleep

> As soon as I get to school, I buy a cup of coffee in the cafeteria.

Some verbs in English are made up of two words. They are called *phrasal verbs*.

Some phrasal verbs can have other words between the two parts of the verb. These are called separable (S) verbs.

I **put on** my coat.   I **put** my coat **on**.

Some phrasal verbs can't be separated.

I **get on** the bus at 7:30 every morning.
NOT   ~~I get the bus on at 7:30 every morning.~~

drop off (S)	get out of	put on (S)
eat out	get up	take off (S)
get in	hang up (S)	turn off (S)
get off	look at	turn on (S)
get on	pick up (S)	wake up (S)

WORD PARTNERSHIPS	
put on	makeup
	a seat belt
	pajamas

A **ACADEMIC** Match each phrasal verb with its meaning.

____f____ **1.** hang up

_____ **2.** get out of

_____ **3.** turn off

_____ **4.** get off

_____ **5.** eat out

_____ **6.** drop off

_____ **7.** get in

_____ **8.** turn on

_____ **9.** pick up

_____ **10.** take off

a. to leave a car or taxi

b. to remove a hat, coat, or other clothing

c. to leave a bus, train, or plane

d. to stop a device or electronic equipment

e. to leave a person at a place

f. to put clothing on a hanger or a hook

g. to eat at a restaurant

h. to start a device or electronic equipment

i. to enter a car or taxi

j. to go somewhere and get someone

B Complete the sentences. Use phrasal verbs.

1. It's raining hard this morning. Can you ____drop____ the children ____off____ at school?

2. It's cold outside. _____ your hat and gloves before you go out.

3. Don't leave your coat on the floor. _____ it _____ in the closet.

4. If you are hot, _____ your sweater.

5. When you _____ the bus, you have to pay the exact fare.

6. I wake up my son at 6:30, but he doesn't _____ until 7:00.

7. I can't see very well. Please _____ the light.

8. I always _____ my children after school.

9. I'm too tired to cook tonight. Let's _____.

C **LET'S TALK.** Read each pair of actions. Explain the order in which you usually do the two actions. Use *before* or *after*.

> I put on my seat belt **after** I start the car.

> Not me. I put on my seat belt **before** I start the car.

put on my seat belt
start the car

wash the dishes
eat dinner

turn off the lights
leave my house

get dressed
eat breakfast

return to my car
the parking meter time expires

eat dinner
do my homework

turn on the computer
check my email

put on my pajamas
go to bed

sharpen my pencil
come to class

turn off the light
get into bed

D Listen to your teacher and complete the sentences. Your teacher will refer to Appendix D in the back of the book.

Mimi has a difficult time falling asleep at night. She gets in bed and puts her head on the pillow. But _____ 1, she begins to worry—about her job, her health, and her family. So, she now has a routine to relax herself _____ 2. _____ 3, she drinks a cup of hot herbal tea. Then, she brushes her teeth. _____ 4, she washes her face and puts on her favorite face cream. _____ 5, she picks up a magazine and reads for a few minutes. Then, she listens to some quiet music. _____ 6, she falls asleep more easily.

Drinking tea before bed can help you sleep.

A Discuss the words and phrases.

buckle	drop off	jump out of	put on
climb into	get dressed	look at	wake up

B Look at the pictures and listen to Matt and Ava's morning routine. 🎧63

1.

2.

3.

4.

5.

6.

7.

8.

9.

C Complete each sentence with the correct form of one of the verbs from the box.

1. Matt _____gets up_____ at 5:45 in the morning.
2. He _____ bed when the alarm clock rings.
3. He _____ Ava after he takes a shower.
4. Matt _____ a movie for the boys.
5. Ava _____ after she eats breakfast.
6. The boys _____ their car seats.
7. Ava _____ the boys into their car seats.
8. She _____ the boys at the daycare center.

> buckle
> climb into
> drop off
> get dressed
> ~~get up~~
> jump out of
> put on
> wake up

D **ACADEMIC** Complete the sentences. Use *before*, *after*, *when*, or *as soon as*. For some sentences, more than one answer is possible.

1. ___After / As soon as / When___ the alarm rings, Matt gets up.
2. Matt takes a shower _____ Ava gets up.
3. _____ Matt gets out of the shower, he wakes Ava up.
4. _____ the boys wake up, they watch a movie.
5. Matt says goodbye to everyone _____ he leaves for work.
6. _____ everyone is ready, they leave.
7. The kids always climb into their car seats _____ they get into the car.
8. Ava's customers don't get angry _____ she's late for work.

E Answer the questions with a partner.

1. Who gets up first?
2. What time does Matt get up?
3. When does he wake Ava up?
4. What does Ava do after she wakes up?
5. When does Ava eat breakfast with the boys?
6. When does Ava get dressed?
7. What does Ava do before she starts the car?
8. Where does Ava take the kids before she goes to work?
9. Why aren't Ava's customers annoyed when she is a little late?

Before- and After-School Care

Childcare is one of the biggest concerns and biggest expenses for working families today. Most single parents work. In 61% of families with two parents, both parents work. About half of school-age children in the United States need care before and/or after school. There is after-school care for many children, but many others go home to empty houses.

In many families with working parents, grandparents and other family members are the ones who take children to school and pick them up after classes end. This type of care works for families because children are comfortable with their relatives and have time to play, talk, and do homework. This care is often free. In some families, one person with a small child may stay home and watch the children of other family members. In these families, the parents often pay something for the childcare. For other families, neighbors and friends help with after-school care.

About 25% of children attend after-school programs. The **majority** of these programs are at public schools. The others are at YMCAs, Boys and Girls Clubs, local recreation centers, and religious organizations. For programs at other locations, a van or bus is needed to pick up the children and bring them to the site. When programs do not offer this service, children of working parents do not have the transportation they need.

As of 2018, more than ten million children attend after-school programs, but there are not enough programs. Over nineteen million more children would **participate** if there were programs in their area.

The cost of an after-school program varies depending on the neighborhood where the program is located and what kinds of activities are provided. Average costs can range between $50 and $100 per week, for one child. Many families **qualify** for government help to pay for these programs. Also, these programs offer tax **advantages** for many families when they file their income taxes.

It's not always easy to find information about after-school programs. Parents can ask the child's school about programs in the area, or call their local recreation department because many offer their own programs. Another great resource is the YMCA or Boys and Girls Clubs, which often have activities for middle school and high school students. Parents can also go online to see if any local faith organizations provide care. One of the best sources of information is other parents. Talking to coworkers, neighbors, and the parents of your children's friends can be very helpful.

Good after-school care can help parents relax at work. Most parents are happy with the after-school programs their children attend. These programs offer snacks, physical activities, help with homework, and STEM (science, technology, engineering, and math) activities. Studies show that children who attend good after-school programs have better school attendance, better **behavior**, and better grades. 🎧 **64**

Children play in the Lions Park Playscape, in Alabama.

A Discuss these questions. Then, read the article on the previous page.

1. Do you know any working families with children? How old are the children?
2. Who cares for the children before and after school?

B Match. Then, complete the sentences.

_____ **1.** majority   **a.** to take part in an activity

_____ **2.** participate   **b.** to meet the requirements for; to be eligible for

_____ **3.** qualify   **c.** a way someone acts

_____ **4.** advantages   **d.** more than half of a group

_____ **5.** behavior   **e.** good things about something; benefits

1. Some children __participate__ in sports after school.
2. My son's teacher is happy because he has good _____ at school.
3. The _____ of working parents need after-school care for their children.
4. Many families _____ for tax benefits related to after-school care.
5. After-school programs offer many _____ for working parents.

> **READING NOTE**
>
> **Identifying Supporting Ideas and Reasons**
>
> Informational texts have one or more main ideas. The text gives reasons or details to support each main idea.

C In your notebook, write reasons or details that support each of these main ideas from the article about community resources on the previous page.

1. Family care is a good choice for many children. *Children are comfortable with their relatives.*
2. Many children can't participate in after-school programs.
3. After-school programs offer many advantages for working families.

D **AT WORK** Check the true statement(s) based on information from the article.

1. In 61% of families with two parents, both parents work.
   - ☐ **a.** In most families with two parents, only one parent works.
   - ☐ **b.** In most families with two parents, both parents work.
2. About 25% of children attend after-school programs.
   - ☐ **a.** Most children attend after-school programs.
   - ☐ **b.** Most children do not attend after-school programs.

A Discuss these questions.

1. Do you ever write short notes or emails? If so, who do you write to?

2. Do you have any children in school? Do you have to write a note or an email when they are absent from school?

B Read the notes to a teacher.

February 10

Dear Ms. Toma,

Please excuse Melissa's absence from class last week. She had the flu. Melissa missed a lot of classwork and homework. Please give her the assignments so she can complete the work at home. Thank you,

Paula Romero

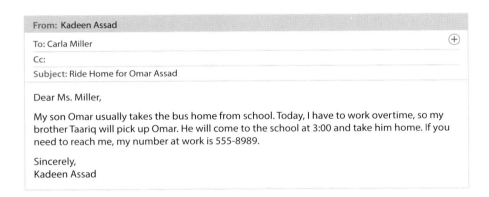

From: **Kadeen Assad**

To: Carla Miller   ⊕

Cc:

Subject: **Ride Home for Omar Assad**

Dear Ms. Miller,

My son Omar usually takes the bus home from school. Today, I have to work overtime, so my brother Taariq will pick up Omar. He will come to the school at 3:00 and take him home. If you need to reach me, my number at work is 555-8989.

Sincerely,
Kadeen Assad

October 10

Dear Mr. Evans,

When my daughter came home yesterday, she was crying. When she was playing outside at recess, a girl pushed her. Another girl pulled her hair. My daughter does not know the names of the girls. She said they are older and in another class. Can you please talk to my daughter and to the older girls? My daughter is very upset. Thank you.

Julie Lin

C Write the reason for each note in Exercise B.

1. Her child was absent from school. The child needs the homework assignments.

2.

3.

WRITING NOTE

Writing a Note to a Teacher

Notes to teachers should be short and specific.

- Do not include unnecessary information.
- Include the date.
- Spell the teacher's name correctly. Use *Mr.* for a *man* and *Ms.* for a *woman*.
- Sign your full name.

D Edit the note. Add any missing information. Cross out any unnecessary sentences.

Dear Ms. Yang,

    My son Victor has an appointment at the doctor on Wednesday at 9:00. I will bring him to school immediately after the appointment. This was the only time available. I am sorry that he will be late tomorrow. You are a very good teacher, and Victor is very happy in your class. Thank you.

Tamara Lapinsky

E **CIVICS** Write a note to a teacher. You have a parent-teacher conference on Monday night at 7:00, but you work at night. Suggest a different day and time for the conference.

F In a small group, read your notes. Which note does the group like best? Why?

A Discuss these questions.

1. When you were a child, how often did you receive a report card?

2. How often do children receive report cards today? Do parents have to sign them?

B **CIVICS** Look at the report card and answer the questions.

WASHINGTON MIDDLE SCHOOL
Student Progress Report

Student: Claudia Figueroa   **Student ID:** 123-12-123   **Grade:** 8

Attendance	Q1	Q2	Q3	Q4
Absent	5	3		
Tardy	4	6		

Subject	Q1	Q2	Q3	Q4	Teacher's Comment
English	B	C			Always cooperative; often late for class; fails to complete assignments; needs extra help
Spanish 2	A	B			Follows directions well; good class participation
Geography	D	C			Improved skills; disorganized work; rarely asks for help; good class participation
Social Studies	C	D			Always cooperative; more study required; disorganized work; rarely asks for help
Algebra 1	C	D			Performs poorly on tests; rarely asks for help; needs extra help; conference needed
Physical Education	B	B			
Computer Science	B	B			Always cooperative; excellent effort; very good work
Art	A	A			Very good work

A = Excellent   B = Good   C = Fair   D = Having Difficulty   F = Failing

1. What grade is Claudia in?

2. What does *tardy* mean?

3. How many times was Claudia absent in the second quarter?

4. What is Claudia's best subject?

5. What subjects are difficult for Claudia?

6. In which subject is Claudia improving?

C Look at the teacher's comments on Claudia's report card. In your notebook, write Claudia's problems. Then, write a suggestion to help Claudia solve each problem.

A pickpocket steals this woman's wallet while she tries to get a taxi.

ACADEMIC Understand a sequence of events; recall and retell information

AT WORK Discuss the role of authorities in a criminal investigation

CIVICS Learn about jury duty

A Discuss each kind of crime.

1. Crime: shoplifting
   Person: shoplifter
   Action: shoplift, steal

2. Crime: mugging
   Person: mugger
   Action: mug, steal

3. Crime: robbery, burglary
   Person: robber, burglar
   Action: steal (a thing),
           rob (a place, person)

4. Crime: car theft
   Person: car thief
   Action: steal

B Discuss these questions with a partner.

1. Have you ever been the victim of a crime? What happened?
2. Was the person who committed the crime found?

A Listen to Jonathan make a statement to a police officer about a robbery at his apartment. Write the things the thief stole. 🎧65

1. _____ 2. _____ 3. _____
4. _____ 5. _____

B Complete the sentences. Use verbs from the box. One of the verbs is negative. Some of the verbs can be used more than once.

be	find	go	leave	lock	open	realize	thank	try	walk

1. When Jonathan _____left_____ his apartment, it was 8:30.

2. Jonathan _____ his door when he _____ his apartment this morning.

3. Before Jonathan _____ to bed last night, he _____ the windows.

4. Jonathan thinks that he _____ the windows before he _____ to work.

5. Jonathan _____ that something was wrong as soon as he _____ to put his keys on the table.

6. When Jonathan _____ into the living room, there _____ a big empty space where his TV used to be.

7. When Jonathan _____ the refrigerator, he _____ his leftover Chinese food.

8. Jonathan _____ the police officer before she _____.

Crime **193**

I locked my door **before** I went to work.   **Before** I went to work, I locked my door.
(main clause)   (time clause)   (time clause)   (main clause)

1. A past time clause explains when an action happened. It usually begins with a time word such as *when*, *before*, *after*, or *as soon as*. A time clause has a subject and a verb.

2. A time clause can come at the beginning or the end of a sentence. If the time clause is at the beginning of a sentence, use a comma (,) after the time clause.

C **Pronunciation: Word stress** Listen and repeat. Pay attention to the words in **bold**. 🎧66

1. Before I **left** my **house**, I **locked** the **door**.
2. When we **went** on **vacation**, we **stopped** the **mail**.
3. She **turned on** the **alarm** before she **left** her **apartment**.
4. They **closed** all the **windows** before they **left**.
5. I **called** the **police** as soon as I **saw** the **broken door**.
6. I **dialed 911** when I **heard** a **noise downstairs**.
7. After **someone robbed** their **house**, they **bought** a **dog**.

	WORD PARTNERSHIPS
break into	a house
	an apartment
	a car

D Listen and complete the conversation. 🎧67

A: You don't look very happy. What's the matter?

B: _____

A: Really? How did they get in?

B: _____

A: Oh. What did they take?

B: _____

A: Did you call the police?

B: _____

E **LET'S TALK.** With a partner, write a conversation about a robbery. Then, act out your conversation.

F Combine the sentences. Yesterday, John and Sue visited their friends. They did not know that a thief was watching their car.

1. John and Sue found a parking space. They parked their car. (when)

    When John and Sue found a parking space, they parked their car.

2. They locked their car. They walked away. (before)

    _____

3. The thief looked around carefully. The couple left. (after)

    _____

4. He didn't see anyone. He walked to the car. (when)

    _____

5. He touched the car. A large dog jumped up and began to bark. (as soon as)

    _____

6. The thief ran away. He saw the dog. (when)

    _____

G **LET'S TALK.** Choose eight of the phrases. Tell a partner about events in your life. Use *before*, *after*, or *when*.

> After I saved enough money, I bought a house.

> Before I got my driver's license, I went to a driving school.

became a citizen	found a job	got my driver's license
bought a house	found an apartment	got robbed
came to this country	got a visa	graduated from college
enrolled in English classes	got divorced	graduated from high school
fell in love	got married	had a baby

I			You		
He	**was**	sleep**ing.**	We	**were**	work**ing.**
She			They		
It		work**ing.**			

> The past continuous describes an action that was in progress at a specific time in the past.

A Complete the sentences. Use the past continuous form of the verbs. What was happening at 4:00 yesterday afternoon?

1. Yesterday at 4:00 p.m., I (drive) _____ *was driving* _____ home from work.
2. I (listen) _____ to the radio.
3. My wife (shop) _____ at the supermarket.
4. My children (study) _____ at the library.
5. You (sleep) _____.
6. My neighbors (watch) _____ TV.
7. Three police officers (investigate) _____ a bank robbery.
8. A thief (climb) _____ through my window!

B **LET'S TALK.** In groups of three, ask and answer the questions about your activities last weekend. Take notes.

	Student 1	Student 2
Where were you on Friday night?		
What were you doing?		
Where were you on Saturday morning?		
What were you doing?		
Where were you on Saturday afternoon?		
What were you doing?		
Where were you on Saturday evening?		
What were you doing?		
Where were you on Sunday afternoon?		
What were you doing?		

/ Past Continuous with *While*

While I **was driving** to school, I **was listening** to the radio. I **was listening** to the radio **while** I **was driving** to school. **While** the professor **was talking**, the students **were taking** notes. The students **were taking** notes **while** the professor **was talking**.	Use *while* with the past continuous to show that two actions were happening at the same time.

A   Complete the sentences. Use your own ideas.

1.   While I was walking to school today, I <u>was talking on my cellphone</u>_____.
2.   While the teacher was returning the tests, the students _____.
3.   While the class was listening to the teacher, I _____.
4.   The boss _____ while the employees _____.
5.   While I was taking the bus to school, I _____.
6.   While Mr. Green was vacuuming the living room, Mrs. Green _____.
7.   I _____ while I was studying.
8.   My friend _____ while I was watching TV.

B   With a partner, take turns making sentences with *while* and the past continuous.

1.   I / cook dinner   I / listen to some music
2.   neighbors / have a party   I / try to sleep
3.   He / watch TV   he / cook dinner
4.   She / walk in the park   she / talk to her friend
5.   I / do my homework   the baby / cry
6.   He / talk on his phone   he / drive
7.   you / watch TV   I / take a nap
8.   I / cook dinner   my daughter / set the table
9.   You / work   I / apply for a job
10. I / enter the building   many students / leave

> While I was cooking dinner, I was listening to music.

> The past continuous can describe an action that was interrupted.
> One action was going on when another action happened.
>   While I **was sleeping**, I **heard** someone in my living room.
>   I **was shopping** in the mall when a thief **stole** my car.

A Complete the sentences. Use the verbs in parentheses.

1. I (watch) _____was watching_____ TV when a man (look) _____looked_____ in my window.

2. We (sit) _____ in class when the fire alarm (ring) _____.

3. A shoplifter (steal) _____ a tablet when the security guard (see) _____ her.

4. While the security guard (take) _____ a break, two men (rob) _____ the jewelry store.

5. Someone (steal) _____ my car while I (work) _____.

6. While I (drive) _____ to work, I (see) _____ an accident.

B In your notebook, write two sentences about each photo. Use *when* or *while*.

While I was on vacation, someone broke into my apartment.

I was on vacation when someone broke into my apartment.

1.

I was on vacation.
Someone broke into my apartment.

2.

Natalie was walking to work.
A man stole her purse.

3.

Thieves were taking the TV.
Tyler called the police.

4.
The driver was speeding.
A police officer pulled him over.

C **ACADEMIC** Read the timeline of the bank robbery. Then, complete the sentences.

2:55	Several customers were in the bank.
2:58	The security guard went on break.
3:00	A robber entered the building. He told everyone to lie down.
3:01	A teller pressed the alarm.
3:02	The robber took $10,000.
3:03	The robber ran out the door. He jumped in his car and drove away.
3:05	The police arrived at the bank. They questioned everyone.

1. Marco was using the ATM machine when _the robber entered the bank._

2. When the robber entered the bank, the security guard _____

3. As soon as the robber entered the bank, _____

4. A teller pressed the alarm when _____

5. Before the robber left the bank, _____

6. The robber ran out before _____

7. While the police were rushing to the bank, _____

8. After the police arrived at the bank, _____

A Last night, Spike and Tina tried to rob a jewelry store. Look at the pictures and listen to the story. 🎧 68

1.
2.
3.
4.

5.
6.
7.
8.

9.
10.
11.
12.

13.
14.
15.
16.

B Match each word with the correct picture from the story. Write the number of the picture. Some words match more than one picture.

_____ arrest	_____ block	_____ fist	_____ take off
_____ mask	_____ break into	_____ get out of	_____ climb into
_____ put on	_____ chase	_____ handcuff	_____ pick up

C **ACADEMIC** Look at the pictures. Tell a partner what you remember about each picture.

D Complete the sentences. Use *before*, *after*, *when*, *while*, or *as soon as*.

1. Spike put on gloves _____ he went into the store.

2. Spike looked around _____ he entered the store.

3. Spike took some jewelry _____ he got into the store.

4. _____ Spike was robbing the store, Tina was sitting in the car.

5. The alarm rang _____ Spike dropped his bag.

6. Tina started the car _____ she heard the alarm.

7. The police officers handcuffed Spike and Tina _____ they put them into the police car.

E Circle *True* or *False*.

1. Spike put on gloves after he broke the window.	True	False
2. Spike climbed into the store after he broke the window.	True	False
3. While Spike was looking around the store, the police arrived.	True	False
4. When Spike saw the pizza, the alarm rang.	True	False
5. Before Spike left the store, he took some jewelry.	True	False
6. As soon as Spike saw the police car, he tried to run away.	True	False
7. Spike took off his mask and hat while he was running away.	True	False

F Answer the questions.

1. What did Spike put on while he was going to the store? _____

2. How did Spike break the window? _____

3. What was Tina doing while Spike was in the store? _____

4. What did Spike do as soon as he got into the store? _____

5. What did Spike steal? _____

6. When did Spike see the pizza? _____

7. What happened when he picked up a slice of pizza? _____

8. When did the alarm ring? _____

9. When did the police officer get out of the car? _____

10. What did the police officers do after they arrested Spike and Tina? _____

Serving on a Jury

One of the responsibilities of a US citizen is to serve on a jury. A jury is a group of ten to twelve citizens who decide if an **accused** criminal is **guilty** or not guilty of a crime. The jury members listen to **evidence** and make a decision. Someone accused of a crime has the right to a jury **trial**. This right is written in the United States Constitution, a document of the laws and government of the United States of America.

How does a district select people for jury duty? First, the district sends a **summons**, or written letter to a citizen in the mail. The district court makes a random selection of registered voters, licensed drivers, and tax payers. The citizen must reply to the summons. If the citizen doesn't reply, that person will have to pay a fine.

What are the requirements to serve on a jury? First, the person must be a US citizen and a resident of the district. The person must be at least 18 years old and be physically and mentally able to serve on the jury. The person must not have any criminal **convictions**, but can still serve if they have traffic violations.

Some people do not want to serve on a jury, but the court will only excuse people for certain reasons, such as if the person is a high school student, the person has to take care of someone who cannot take care of him/herself, or if the person does not understand enough English to follow the trial.

If the court selects you for a jury, there are rules that you must follow:

- Do not discuss the case until you hear all of the evidence.
- Do not investigate the case yourself.
- Do not discuss the case with family members or anyone else.
- Listen to the judge's instructions.

If you are selected to sit on a jury, the average trial is one to three days, but trials may be longer. Also, it is possible that you will report for jury duty, but you will not be part of the jury. The district court calls many people, and only a small number can serve on a jury. If, after one or two days, the court does not call you to trial, your service is complete for at least one year. 🎧69

Members of the jury have to take an oath before serving. They have to swear that they will be fair and that they will give a true verdict.

A **CIVICS** After reading, discuss these questions.

1. Do you know anyone who has served on a jury?

2. Have you ever received a jury summons? Did you serve?

B Read and circle the correct answer.

1. A person who is accused of a crime has a right to…
   a. receive a summons.
   b. serve on a jury.
   c. have a jury trial.
   d. decide if a person is guilty or not guilty.

2. The United States Constitution is a…
   a. building in Washington, D.C.
   b. document of the laws and government of the US.
   c. type of trial jury.
   d. list of jury responsibilities.

3. What is the first step in selecting a jury?
   a. Decide if the accused is guilty or not guilty.
   b. Send summonses to citizens of the district.
   c. Listen to the evidence in court.
   d. Pay the fine for jury duty.

4. Which of the following is **not** a requirement for jury service?
   a. You must be at least 18 years old.
   b. You must be a US citizen.
   c. You must have a driver's license.
   d. You must understand English well.

5. Which *two* of the following statements are **false**?
   a. You can talk to your friends about the trial.
   b. You must reply to the jury summons.
   c. Everyone with a summons serves on a jury.
   d. People can be excused from jury duty.

C Complete the sentences with the words from the box.

| accused | convictions | evidence | guilty | ~~summons~~ | trial |

1. Last summer, I received a jury _____summons_____ in the mail.

2. A juror only has to serve on one _____ a year.

3. There was no strong _____ , so the jury said, "Not guilty."

4. The _____ person had a history of past crimes.

5. A jury decides if a person is _____ or not guilty.

6. I am able to serve on a jury because I have no _____ for any crimes.

A Discuss these questions.

1. Have you or anyone you know ever been robbed?

2. Where did the robbery happen? What did the thief take? Was anyone hurt?

B Read Martin's story about a robbery in his neighborhood.

In July 2017, my grandparents and a neighbor were talking in the living room. It was a Saturday night at about 9:00. My grandfather was looking out the window when he saw a large green truck on the street. Ten minutes later, he saw two men. They were wearing brown uniforms. The men were putting a sofa, two armchairs, and a coffee table in the truck. Then, he saw them putting two TVs, a bed, and a dresser into the truck. He asked my grandmother and the neighbor, "Are Maria and Pablo moving?"

As soon as the neighbor saw the men, he said, "They're thieves!" My grandmother called 911. My grandfather ran out of the house and got into his car with the neighbor. My grandfather and the neighbor drove after the thieves, but the thieves' truck was faster than my grandfather's car, so they couldn't catch them. The police were no help because they arrived ten minutes later.

When the owners of the house, Maria and Pablo, came back from the beach, my grandfather said, "I'm sorry. I saw what happened, but I couldn't stop them. My car is too slow."

Maria and Pablo said, "I'm glad you didn't catch the thieves. Don't worry. Our furniture was very old. The insurance will pay for new furniture."

My grandfather was surprised. He said, "I will never risk my life again for problems that aren't mine."

C Rewrite each sentence with the proper punctuation and capitalization.

1. The robber said give me your wallet

   The robber said, "Give me your wallet."

2. The police officer asked did you lock your door this morning

   _____

3. I answered yes. I always lock the door in the morning

   _____

4. A woman on the street shouted help

   _____

5. The store owner said I'm going to call the police

   _____

D **ACADEMIC** You are going to write about a crime that happened to you or that you heard or read about. Plan your writing so that it includes these important facts:

1. Who did the crime happen to? _____

2. Who committed the crime? _____

3. What was the crime? _____

4. When did the crime happen? _____

5. Where did it happen? _____

E In your notebook, write about the crime. Use the information in Exercise D. Include one or two quotations in your story.

F Read your story to a partner. Your partner will ask you more questions about the crime.

G **AT WORK** Discuss these questions with your partner.

1. Did any authorities investigate the crime you wrote about?

2. What did the officer(s) do during the investigation?

3. Did the authorities solve the case? How?

A **CIVICS** Complete each definition with a word or phrase from the photo.

1. The _____*judge*_____ is the person in charge of the court.

2. The _____ is the person charged with a crime.

3. The _____ is the lawyer for the defendant. He / She tries to show that the defendant is innocent—that is, not guilty.

4. The _____ is the person who files a legal complaint against another person.

5. The _____ is the lawyer for the plaintiff. He / She tries to prove that the defendant is guilty.

6. A _____ is a person who brings information to the court about a crime.

7. The _____ is the group of people who sits in court and decides if a person is guilty.

CULTURE NOTE

When the police arrest a person, they must read the person his or her rights:

"You have the right to remain silent. Anything you say can and will be used against you in a court of law. You have the right to speak to an attorney and have an attorney present during any questioning. If you cannot afford a lawyer, one will be provided for you at government expense."

An engineer stands at the top of a wind turbine. His "office" sits at 220 feet in the air.

AT WORK Talk about career goals; discuss education requirements for certain jobs; create a resume; research jobs

ACADEMIC Scan text for important information

CIVICS Research careers and statistics using online US government resources

A Write the name of the job under each picture.

1. _____

2. _____

3. _____

4. _____

5. _____

6. _____

B **AT WORK** Discuss these questions.

1. Would you like to have one of the jobs in the photos? If so, which one?
2. Where would you like to work—in an office or outside?
3. Would you like to supervise other people?
4. What kind of job did you have before coming to this country?
5. What job would you like to have in the future?
6. What kind of education do you need?

C AT WORK Write each occupation under the education it requires. Some occupations fit in more than one category.

Occupations	Education Required
carpenter	**Professional Degree**
chef	1. _____
computer engineer	2. _____
dental hygienist	3. _____
dentist	**Bachelor's Degree (Four-year college)**
electrician	1. _____
emergency medical technician (EMT)	2. _____
hairstylist	3. _____
home health aide	4. _____
lawyer	**Associate's Degree (Two-year college)**
licensed practical nurse (LPN)	1. _____
machine operator	2. _____
manicurist	3. _____
physical therapist	**Vocational Training**
physician	1. _____
plumber	2. _____
registered nurse (RN)	3. _____
respiratory therapist	4. _____
secondary school teacher	**Learn on the job / Short-term training**
social worker	1. _____
	2. _____
	3. _____
	4. _____
	5. _____
	6. _____

WORD PARTNERSHIPS	
college	
associate's	
bachelor's	degree
master's	
professional	

She **will go** to college after she **graduates** from high school.
    (main clause)   (time clause)

After she **graduates** from high school, she **will go** to college.
         (time clause)   (main clause)

Notes:

1. A time clause begins with words such as *if, before, after, as soon as,* and *when*. A time clause has a subject and a verb.

2. The verb in the main clause is in the future (with *will* or *be going to*). The verb in the time clause is in the present.

3. A time clause can be at the beginning or at the end of a sentence.

A Match.

_____*b*____ **1.** If I do well in my English course,

_____ **2.** After Julia completes her engineering degree,

_____ **3.** When Frank becomes a nurse,

_____ **4.** Before Rick applies to the police department,

_____ **5.** If I receive a good evaluation,

_____ **6.** After Laura finishes high school,

_____ **7.** Before I go to the job interview,

a. he will need to take a physical exam.

b. I will become an interpreter.

c. she'll enter a community college.

d. I will research the company.

e. she'll design cars.

f. I will get a promotion.

g. he will have to give medication.

B Listen to your teacher and complete the sentences. Your teacher will refer to Appendix D in the back of the book.

1. Maria _____ for a job before she _____.

2. Before she _____ for a job, she _____ her resume.

3. She _____ out her resume when she _____ a good job posting.

4. If she _____ of a job opening, she _____ the company.

5. When she _____ on an interview, she _____ a suit.

6. If she _____ a good impression, the company _____ her.

C Complete the sentences about Bernato. He would like to open his own restaurant someday.

1. After Bernato (graduate) _____graduates_____ from high school, he (go) _____will go_____ to culinary school.

2. When he (go) _____ to culinary school, he (work) _____ in a restaurant part time.

3. Bernato (take) _____ a few business classes after he (graduate) _____ from culinary school.

4. Bernato (work) _____ in a restaurant for several years after he (finish) _____ his education.

5. When he (decide) _____ to open a restaurant, he (discuss) _____ his plans with his family.

6. If he (have – negative) _____ enough money, he (apply) _____ for a bank loan.

7. He (look) _____ for a good location when he (be) _____ ready to open a restaurant.

D **AT WORK** Use the words below to write sentences about Miguel.

1. When / Miguel's company / close   he / apply for / unemployment benefits
   When Miguel's company closes, he will apply for unemployment benefits.

2. After / he / get laid off   he / register for night classes
   _____

3. When / his friend / have / extra work   Miguel / help him
   _____

4. Miguel's wife / work / full time   when / Miguel / get laid off
   _____

5. When / his wife / be / at work   Miguel / take care of / the children
   _____

E Read about this career.

Bookkeeping, Accounting, and Auditing Clerks

What They Do

Bookkeeping, accounting, and auditing clerks are financial record keepers. They record financial transactions, update statements, and check financial records.

How to Become a Bookkeeping, Accounting, and Auditing Clerk

Most bookkeeping, accounting, and auditing clerks have some college education, especially courses in accounting. Experience with spreadsheets and bookkeeping software is required. Also, new clerks often receive on-the-job training from experienced employees.

Pay

In 2016 the median annual salary of bookkeeping, accounting, and auditing clerks was $38,390.

Job Outlook

There will be little change in the number of bookkeepers, accountants, and auditors needed by companies from 2016 to 2026.

F **AT WORK** Complete with the correct form of the verbs in parentheses.

Lian wants to be a bookkeeper. At this time, Lian (work) _____ in the shipping department of a company. At night, she (study) _____ English. When she (complete) _____ her English classes, Lian (apply) _____ to the community college near her home. She (take) _____ courses in accounting. She (continue) _____ to work full time while she (study) _____ accounting. After she (take) _____ a few classes, she (look) _____ for an entry-level job in accounting. She (earn) _____ her associate's degree in accounting in three years. After she (complete) _____ her degree, she (apply) _____ for a promotion at work.

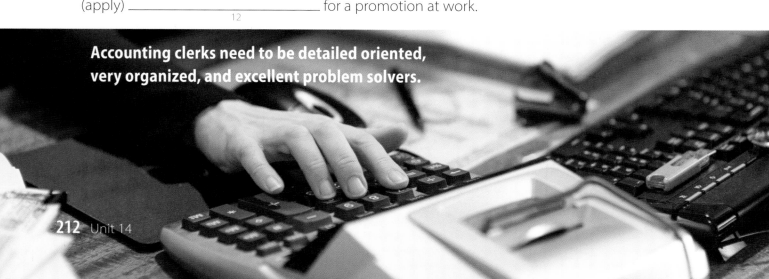

Accounting clerks need to be detailed oriented, very organized, and excellent problem solvers.

G Read about this career.

Physical Therapy Assistants

What They Do

Physical therapy assistants work under the supervision of physical therapists. They help people who are recovering from injuries and illnesses improve their movement. Most physical therapy assistants work in physical therapy offices or hospitals.

How to Become a Physical Therapy Assistant

Physical therapy assistants need an associate's degree from an accredited program. They must have a license or a certificate.

Pay

In 2016, the median annual salary for physical therapy assistants was $56,610.

Job Outlook

Experts think the employment for physical therapy assistants will grow by 30 percent from 2016 to 2026, much faster than many other occupations.

H **AT WORK** Listen to Jessica's career plans. Take notes. Then, answer the questions. 🎧70

_____

_____

_____

_____

_____

_____

1. Where does Jessica live?
2. What is she studying now?
3. What program is she going to begin when she completes these classes?
4. Is she going to work while she attends the program?
5. What is she going to do before she begins the program?
6. How many years is the program?
7. Who is going to help Jessica with expenses?
8. What kind of experience is Jessica going to get before she graduates?
9. When will she apply for a job?
10. How much money will she earn after she graduates?

A physical therapist works with a patient.

What **are** you **going to do** after you **graduate**?   Where **is** he **going to live** if his company **transfers** him?   When he **starts** school, **is** he **going to work** full time?

In a question with a future time clause, use the future question form in the main clause.

A Pronunciation: Question Intonation Listen and repeat. 🎧 71

1. What are you going to do if you win the lottery?

2. What will you do after you finish this class?

3. If she gets a promotion, what is she going to buy?

4. When he finishes college, where will he work?

B Answer the questions.

1. What are they going to do if they win the lottery?

   _____

   _____

2. What is she going to do if she gets laid off?

   _____

   _____

3. What are they going to do if it starts to rain?

   _____

   _____

4. What is he going to buy if he gets a promotion?

   _____

   _____

C Ask and answer the questions with a partner.

1. What are you going to do today when you finish this class?
2. What are you going to do if you go back to the country where you were born?
3. What career will you study when you finish your English classes?
4. When you finish your classes, where will you work?
5. What will you do when your friends come to visit?
6. What are you going to do if you win the lottery?

D Listen to the conversation. Then, practice it with a partner. 🎧72

A: What are your plans for next year?

B: I'm going to finish my English classes.

A: What are you going to do when you finish your classes?

B: When I finish my English classes, I'm going to enter nursing school.

A: Where are you going to work after you graduate?

B: I'm going to work in the emergency room of a hospital.

E Write down your plans for the future.

My Plans

F **LET'S TALK.** Tell a partner about your future plans. Then, write a conversation about your plans. Act out your conversation for the class.

A **AT WORK** The chart presents three medical careers. Listen and complete the information. 🎧73

Career	Phlebotomist	Occupational Therapy Assistant	Surgical Technician
Training/Education	Most need a professional _____, or on-the-job _____	An _____ degree; _____ weeks of hands-on experience; courses in: _____, _____, and health education	_____ college or vocational school program
Salary (2016)	$32,710	$ _____	$ _____
Job Outlook	_____%	_____ %	_____%
Job Responsibilities	Draw _____; _____ patient feel comfortable; _____ information into a computer	_____ patients how to use equipment; work closely with the _____	Prepare the _____ room for surgery; sterilize _____; _____ patients for surgery

An occupational therapist practices an exercise with a patient.

B Listen again. Circle the correct answer. 🎧73

1. Ronaldo doesn't want to…

   a. work with people. b. work in a hospital. c. study for a long time.

2. Ronaldo wants a job that…

   a. will keep him busy. b. will allow him to work part time. c. will be easy.

3. Ronaldo would be a good phlebotomist because he…

   a. doesn't need any training. b. is good with people. c. wants an easy job.

4. If Ronaldo studies to become an occupational therapist, he may not have to…

   a. take any other courses. b. take biology or psychology. c. take health education.

5. Ronaldo has a _____ who is a surgical technician.

   a. neighbor b. friend c. relative

C Listen and circle the job(s) that fits each description. 🎧74

1. **a.** Phlebotomist **b.** Occupational therapy assistant **c.** Surgical technician

2. **a.** Phlebotomist **b.** Occupational therapy assistant **c.** Surgical technician

3. **a.** Phlebotomist **b.** Occupational therapy assistant **c.** Surgical technician

4. **a.** Phlebotomist **b.** Occupational therapy assistant **c.** Surgical technician

5. **a.** Phlebotomist **b.** Occupational therapy assistant **c.** Surgical technician

6. **a.** Phlebotomist **b.** Occupational therapy assistant **c.** Surgical technician

7. **a.** Phlebotomist **b.** Occupational therapy assistant **c.** Surgical technician

D Discuss these questions.

1. Which career do you think Ronaldo should choose? Why?

2. Which career do you think you would like best? Why?

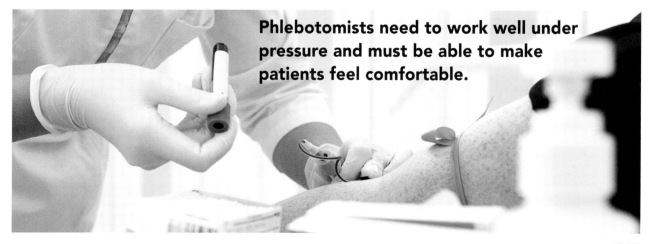

Phlebotomists need to work well under pressure and must be able to make patients feel comfortable.

Automotive Service Technicians and Mechanics

What Automotive Service Technicians and Mechanics Do

Automotive service technicians and mechanics, often called *service technicians* or *service techs*, inspect, maintain, and repair cars and light trucks. Basic repairs include changing oil, checking fluid levels and rotating tires. Service technicians identify problems, often by using computerized equipment. In large shops, automotive technicians specialize in different types of repairs, such as brakes or air conditioning.

Work Environment

Almost 60% of technicians work for automobile dealers or in repair shops. Another 13% are self-employed. Most dealers and shops are well-ventilated and well-lit. Technicians commonly work with greasy parts and tools, sometimes in uncomfortable positions. Workplace injuries, such as small cuts, sprains, and bruises are common.

How to Become an Automotive Service Technician or Mechanic

High school courses in automotive repair provide a good background, but employees prefer that automotive service technicians and mechanics complete an automotive technology program at a postsecondary institution. Industry certification is usually required once the person is employed.

Pay

The median annual wage for automotive service technicians and mechanics was $39,550 in May 2017. Technicians at automotive dealers usually earn more than technicians at repair shops.

Job Outlook

Employment of automotive service technicians and mechanics is projected to grow 6% from 2016 to 2026, about as fast as the average for all occupations. There should be many job opportunities for qualified technicians. 🎧75

Source: Bureau of Labor Statistics, U.S. Department of Labor, *Occupational Outlook Handbook*, Automotive Service Technicians and Mechanics, on the Internet at https://www.bls.gov/ooh/installation-maintenance-and-repair/automotive-service-technicians-and-mechanics.htm (*November 06, 2017*).

Two mechanics inspect parts of a car.

Quick Facts	
2017 Median Pay	$39,550 per year $19.02 per hour
Typical Entry-Level Education	Postsecondary nondegree award
Work Experience in a Related Occupation	None
On-the-job Training	Short-term
Number of Jobs, 2016	749,900
Job Outlook, 2016-26	6% (As fast as average)
Employment Change, 2016-26	45,900

The *Occupational Outlook Handbook* is an online career guide published by the United States Department of Labor. You can find current information on hundreds of careers:

- Explanations of exactly what people do at each job
- Descriptions of work environments
- The training and education needed for each career
- Pay information
- The job outlook, or number of jobs in the future, for each career

A **ACADEMIC** Scan the Quick Facts box and the article about automotive service technicians. Underline the correct answers to these questions.

1. What was the median pay for automotive technicians in 2017?
2. How many more automotive workers will be needed by 2026?
3. Where do most service technicians work?
4. What is one negative of this work?
5. What education do most automotive dealers and shops prefer?
6. What is the job outlook for the future?

READING NOTE

Scanning for Information
Sometimes it is not necessary to read every word. You can scan the text, looking at the text quickly to find specific information you need.

B **AT WORK** Go online and research a career that interests you. Take notes about the career you choose.

1. Career: _____
2. Job Description: _____
3. Education Required: _____
4. Job Outlook: _____
5. Pay: _____

C Listen to other students describe the careers they researched to the class. Write two careers that interest you.

Diego Medina
937 Franklin Lane
Red Bank, NJ 07701
732-555-6347
dmedina@call*me.com

Put your name, address, telephone number, and email address at the top of the resume.

Career Objective:

To pursue a career as a paralegal in the public or private sector; to use my experience conducting case research, and collecting and analyzing evidence for attorney use.

Explain the kind of job you are looking for.

Education:

Essex County College, Newark, NJ
A.A.S. in Paralegal Studies, GPA 3.6, May 2017

Write the names of the schools you attended and the date you graduated.

Employment History:

• Lord and Robbins, P.C. Personal and Injury Law, 2015 to present
  Conduct case research, organize and track files
• Paner and Elliot, LLC, Criminal Law Intern, summer 2016
  Maintained reference files for ongoing cases
• County Court, Intake Intern, 2015
  Obtained intake information on juveniles

List the jobs you have had and your responsibilities. Write your resume in reverse chronological order, from the present to the past.

Activities:

Paralegal Club, Essex County College,
Paralegal Association of New Jersey

Name activities and organizations you belong to.

Skills:

Computer experience with legal software
Languages: fluent Spanish, advanced Portuguese

List your computer skills, languages you can speak, and other skills you have.

A Prepare to write your resume. Complete the information.

Career Objective:

_____

_____

_____

Education: (Note: Start with the name of your current school.)

_____

_____

_____

Employment History: (Note: Start with your current job.)

_____

_____

_____

Activities:

_____

_____

_____

Skills:

_____

_____

_____

B Use your notes and write your resume. Follow the form on the previous page.

WRITING NOTE
Editing a Resume
1. Type your resume.
2. Ask a teacher or counselor to proofread your resume.
3. Review all the dates on your resume.

ENGLISH IN ACTION / Researching a Career

CIVICS In the United States, students use many resources to think about their careers. Some of these resources are:

1. Career counselors at high schools and colleges
2. Career books and online career resources
3. Volunteer jobs and part-time work
4. Job fairs – Events at schools or other locations where professionals give information and advice about their careers.
5. Talking to people in the kind of work you are interested in

A LET'S TALK. Talk about your skills and interests with a partner. Check your skills and your partner's skills.

Skills	You	Your Partner
1. I am artistic. I like to draw and design things.		
2. I am good at math. I like to work with numbers.		
3. I like to teach people how to do things.		
4. I like to operate and drive vehicles.		
5. I like science and solving problems.		
6. I like to read and write and work with information.		
7. I like to work with computers and software programs.		
8. I like to repair and maintain machines.		
9. I like to entertain people. I can sing, dance, or play an instrument.		
10. I like to help people who are sick.		

B Complete.

1. I like to _____.
2. Two possible careers for me are _____ and _____.
3. My partner likes to _____.
4. Two possible careers for him / her are _____ and _____.

C In your notebook, write the steps you need to take to find a job in the career you researched.

UNIT 1

Simple Present

STATEMENTS		
Subject	Verb	
I	work	every day.
You	work	at night.
We	work	in the morning.
They	work	in a restaurant.
He	work**s**	at a hospital.
She	work**s**	downtown.
It	work**s**	each time.

Notes:

1. The simple present tells about a repeated or routine action.

2. The simple present tells about facts that are true all the time.

   I live in the city.   *I drive to school.*

3. The verb ends in *-s* for affirmative statements with *he, she,* and *it.*

There is / There are

AFFIRMATIVE STATEMENTS
There is a book on the desk.
There are four books on the desk.
There are some books on the desk.

NEGATIVE STATEMENTS
There isn't a book on the desk.
There aren't any books on the desk.

YES / NO QUESTIONS
Is there a map in your classroom?
Are there any maps in your classroom?

SHORT ANSWERS	
Yes, **there is.**	No, **there isn't.**
Yes, **there are.**	No, **there aren't.**

Notes:

1. A sentence beginning with *There is* often shows location.

   There is *a book on the desk.*

2. A sentence beginning with *There are* often tells how many.

   There are *twenty students in our class.*

3. Use *some* in a plural statement in the affirmative. Use *any* in a plural statement in the negative. Use *any* in a plural question.

4. Use *there* the first time you talk about a thing. Use *it* or *they* the second time.

   There *is a book on the desk.*   **It** *is a dictionary.*

   There *are many students in our class.*   **They** *are from different countries.*

QUANTIFIERS		
None One	of us of the students	is married. walks to school.
None A couple Some A few Most All	of us of the students of the children	are married. live in New York.

Note:

None is used with both the singular and the plural form of a verb.

   None *of us* **is** *married.*
   None *of us* **are** *married.*

UNIT 2

Simple Present

AFFIRMATIVE STATEMENTS	
Subject	Verb
I You We They	work.
He She It	works.

NEGATIVE STATEMENTS		
Subject	*Do not / Does not*	Verb
I You We They	do not / don't	work.
He She It	does not / doesn't	

PRESENT TIME EXPRESSIONS

every morning   **once** a week   **on** the weekend   **in** the summer
every day   **twice** a month   **on** Sundays   **in** the winter
every night   **three times** a year

ADVERBS OF FREQUENCY

I **always** wear my seat belt.
I **usually** eat breakfast.
I **frequently** eat out.
I **often** eat out.
I **sometimes** work overtime.
I **hardly ever** get up late.
I **rarely** get up late.
I **never** take a taxi.

Notes:
1. Time expressions usually appear at the end of a sentence.
2. Put adverbs of frequency after the verb *be*.
   *I <u>am</u> **never** late for work.*
   *She <u>is</u> **rarely** sick.*
3. Put adverbs of frequency before other verbs.
   *I **often** <u>walk</u> in the park.*
   *He **never** <u>takes</u> a taxi.*

UNIT 3

Simple Present

YES / NO QUESTIONS			
Do / Does	Subject	Verb	
Do	I you we they	bank have pay	online? a car loan? rent?
Does	he she		
	it	cost	a lot?

SHORT ANSWERS	
Affirmative	Negative
Yes, you **do**. Yes, I **do**. Yes, we **do**. Yes, they **do**.	No, you **don't**. No, I **don't**. No, we **don't**. No, they **don't**.
Yes, he **does**. Yes, she **does**. Yes, it **does**.	No, he **doesn't**. No, she **doesn't**. No, it **doesn't**.

WH-QUESTIONS				**ANSWERS**		
Wh- word	*Do / Does*	Subject	Verb	Subject	Verb	
When	do	I	work?	You	work	at 2:00.
Where	do	you	study?	I	study	at the adult school.
What	do	we	need?	We	need	a computer.
When	do	they	eat?	They	eat	at 7:00.
How much	does	he	save?	He	save**s**	$100 a week.
How	does	she	get to work?	She	take**s**	the bus.

Who Questions

WHO AS A SUBJECT

Who works at City Bank?
Laura does.

Who saves money every month?
Henry and **Ivan** do.

> Note:
>
> When *Who* is the subject of a sentence, it is always singular.

WHO AS AN OBJECT

Who does he drive to work?
He drives **his brother** to work.

Who do they send money to?
They send money **to their parents**.

> Note:
>
> When *Who* is the object of a sentence, it can be singular or plural.

UNIT 4

Count Nouns

SINGULAR	**PLURAL**
a state	states
every state	all the states
each of the states	many of the states

Notes:

1. Count nouns are people, places, or things that we can count individually (one by one). Count nouns can be singular or plural.

2. Expressions with *one of the*, *every*, and *each* are singular.

   Every state **has** a capitol building.

3. Expressions with *a few of the*, *some of the*, *many of the*, *all of the*, etc., are plural.

   All of the states **have** capitol buildings.

QUANTIFIERS WITH COUNT NOUNS

There	is isn't	a	seaport desert	on the coast. in the North.
	are	a few several many a lot of	seaports mountains rivers forests	in the South. in the East. in the West. in the central part
	aren't	any	farms	of the country.

COUNT AND NONCOUNT NOUNS

Count Nouns	Noncount Nouns
a river	rain
mountains	pollution
tourists	tourism

Notes:

1. *Aren't* can also be used with *many* and *a lot of*.

2. Noncount nouns cannot be counted. They are always singular.

- Liquids or gasses: *water, oil, oxygen, rain*
- Items that are too small or too numerous to count: *sand, corn, rice*
- General categories: *traffic, scenery, music, tourism*
- Ideas: *information, beauty, work*
- Some words can be both count and noncount: *crime—crimes, industry—industries*

QUANTIFIERS WITH NONCOUNT NOUNS

There	is	no a little a lot of	traffic rain crime industry	in this city. in my country. in the United States.
	isn't	any much		

HOW MUCH / HOW MANY

How much	snow traffic	is	there	in your city? in your country?
How many	museums parks	are		

Note:

A lot of can be used with *isn't*.

There **isn't a lot of** rain in the desert.

TOO MUCH / TOO MANY / NOT ENOUGH

There	is	too much	rain.
		not enough	industry.
	are	too many	fast-food restaurants.
		not enough	parks.

Note:

We often use *not enough* and *too many / too much* to talk about problems or to complain.

too many, too much = more than you want or need

There are **too many** cars on the road. There is **too much** traffic.

not enough = less than you want or need

There are**n't enough** farms in that country. There is**n't enough** food.

UNIT 5

Present Continuous

STATEMENTS

Subject	*Be*	(not)	*-ing* Form
I	am		sending an email.
You	are		ordering a movie.
He	is		making reservations.
She	is	(not)	typing an essay.
It	is		working.
We	are		texting.
They	are		playing a video game.

Notes:

1. The present continuous talks about an action that is happening now.
   *He **is using** his computer.*
2. The present continuous talks about an action that is temporary.
   *He **is living** with his brother.*   (He expects to move soon.)
3. The present continuous can talk about specific future plans.
   *I'm **leaving** at 2:00.*

YES / NO QUESTIONS

Be	Subject	*-ing* Form
Am	I	taking a picture?
Are	you	sending an email?
Is	she	listening to music?
Is	it	working?
Are	they	making reservations?

SHORT ANSWERS

Affirmative	Negative
Yes, you **are**.	No, you **aren't**. / No, you**'re not**.
Yes, I **am**.	No, I**'m not**.
Yes, she **is**.	No, she **isn't**. / No, she**'s not**.
Yes, it **is**.	No, it **isn't**. / No, it**'s not**.
Yes, they **are**.	No, they **aren't**. / No, they**'re not**.

WH- QUESTIONS

Wh- word	*Be*	Subject	*-ing* Form
What	am	I	doing?
Which movie	are	you	ordering?
How	is	it	working?
Where	are	they	going?

ANSWERS

Subject + Verb
You're checking prices.
I'm ordering *Space Age*.
It's working well.
They're going to the lab.

WHO QUESTIONS

Who	Verb	
Who	is buying	a camera?
Who	is fixing	the computer?

Notes:

1. When *Who* is the subject of a sentence, it is always singular.

Who is buying a camera?	*Laura is.*
Who is working today?	*Sarah and Ali are.*

2. When *Who* is the object of a sentence, it can be singular or plural.

Who is Max calling?	*He is calling his sister.*
Who are they speaking with?	*They are speaking with the customers.*

NONACTION VERBS

hate	feel	agree	belong
like	hear	believe	cost
love	look	forget	have
prefer	see	know	need
	seem	remember	own
	smell	think	
	sound	understand	
	taste		

Notes:

1. Some verbs in English are not used with the present continuous. They are called nonaction verbs. These verbs often show feelings, senses, beliefs, and possession.
2. Some verbs can show both nonaction and action.

*I **have** a computer.*	*I'm **having** a good time.*
	*She's **having** a party.*
*I **think** he's a good teacher.*	*I'm **thinking** about my vacation.*

Future with *Be going to*

STATEMENTS				
Subject	*Be*	*(not)*	*Going to*	Verb
I	am			exercise.
You	are	(not)	going to	make an appointment.
He	is			call the doctor.
They	are			take medication.

YES / NO QUESTIONS			
Be	Subject	*Going to*	Verb
Are	you		see the doctor?
Is	she	going to	stay home from work?
Are	they		get a flu shot?

ANSWERS	
Affirmative	Negative
Yes, I am.	No, I'm not.
Yes, she is.	No, she isn't.
Yes, they are.	No, they aren't.

WH- QUESTIONS				
Wh- word	*Be*	Subject	*Going to*	Verb
When	am	I		
Where	are	you	going to	exercise?
Why	is	he		
	are	they		

Future with *Will*

STATEMENTS		
Subject	*Will / Won't*	Verb
I		walk every day.
You		join a health club.
He	will	change jobs.
She	won't	
We		
They		

Notes:

1. Use *will* to express an offer to help.
   I'll drive you to school.

2. Use *will* to make predictions.
   You'll get the job.

UNIT 7

COMPARATIVE ADJECTIVES

New York is **larger than** Atlanta.
Chicago is **busier than** Denver.
Houston is **more populated than** Boston.

Notes:

1. Comparative adjectives compare two people, places, or things.

2. For one-syllable adjectives, add -er + than.

    tall – taller than   *long – longer than*

3. For one-syllable adjectives ending in a consonant followed by -y, change the -y to -i, and add -er + than.

    dry – drier than

4. For two-syllable adjectives ending in y, change the y to i, and add -er + than.

    busy – busier than   *happy – happier than*

5. For other adjectives with two or more syllables, use *more* + adjective + *than*.

    beautiful – more beautiful than   *populated – more populated than*

6. These comparative adjectives are irregular.

    good – better than   *bad – worse than*   *far – farther than*

MORE / LESS / FEWER + NOUN

New York Los Angeles	has	more fewer	universities jobs	than	Los Angeles. New York.
		more less	traffic noise		

Notes:

1. Use *more* and *less* with noncount nouns.

2. Use *more* and *fewer* with count nouns.

SUPERLATIVE ADJECTIVES

Russia is **the largest** country in the world.
Atlanta Airport is **the busiest** airport in the world.
New York is **the most populated** city in the United States.

Notes:

1. Superlative adjectives compare three or more people, places, or things.

2. For one-syllable adjectives, add *the* + -est.

    tall – the tallest   *long – the longest*

3. For two-syllable adjectives ending in y, change the y to i, and add *the* + est.

    busy – the busiest   *happy – the happiest*

4. For other adjectives with two or more syllables, use *the most* + adjective.

    beautiful – the most beautiful   *populated – the most populated*

5. These superlative adjectives are irregular.

    good – the best   *bad – the worst*   *far – the farthest*

	AS... AS				NOT AS... AS		
China France	is	as interesting as as beautiful as	India. Italy.	Colombia Ecuador	isn't	as populated as as large as	Brazil. Mexico.

Notes:

1. Use *as . . . as* to show that two people, places, or things are the same.
2. Use *not as . . . as* to show that two people, places, or things are not the same.

   Florida is **not as large as** *Texas.* = *Texas is* **larger than** *Florida.*

   Silver is **not as expensive as** *gold.* = *Gold is* **more expensive than** *silver.*

UNIT 8

Simple Past

REGULAR VERBS

I **lived** in Taiwan.
He **moved** to the United States.
They **signed** a lease.

Notes:

1. Regular simple past verbs end in -*d* or -*ed* (See Appendix B).
2. The simple past form is the same for singular and plural subjects.
3. **Irregular** past verbs do not follow the same rules.

PAST TIME EXPRESSIONS

Yesterday	Last	Ago
yesterday morning	last night	a few minutes ago
yesterday afternoon	last week	an hour ago
yesterday evening	last weekend	a week ago
	last Saturday	two years ago
	last month	
	last year	

Note:
Use a past time expression at the beginning or the end of a sentence.

NEGATIVES

I **didn't paint** the bedroom.
We **didn't live** in an apartment.
He **didn't study** English.
She **didn't take** the test.
They **didn't go** to the park.
It **didn't work**.

Note:
Use *didn't* and the simple form of the verb to form the negative past form.

BE

Present	Past
I **am** busy.	I **was** busy.
You **are** lonely.	You **were** lonely.
He **is** friendly.	He **was** friendly.
It **is** safe.	It **was** safe.
We **are** homesick.	We **were** homesick.
They **are** noisy.	They **were** noisy.

Notes:

1. *Was* and *were* are past forms of *be*.
2. The negative form of was is was not / *wasn't*. The negative form of were is were not / *weren't*.

   I **wasn't** *busy.*

   You **weren't** *lonely.*

UNIT 9

BE

Present	Past	
I **am** home.	I **was** home.	I **wasn't** at home.
You **are** at work.	You **were** at work.	You **weren't** at work.
We **are** scared.	We **were** scared.	We **weren't** scared.
They **are** at school.	They **were** at school.	They **weren't** at school.
He **is** cold.	He **was** cold.	He **wasn't** cold.
She **is** upset.	She **was** upset.	She **wasn't** upset.
It **is** windy.	It **was** windy.	It **wasn't** windy.

Simple Past

YES / NO QUESTIONS

Did	Subject	Verb
	you	**evacuate**?
Did	he	**go** to work?
	it	**rain** all week?
	they	**lose** power?

SHORT ANSWERS

Affirmative	Negative
Yes, I **did**.	No, I **didn't**.
Yes, he **did**.	No, he **didn't**.
Yes, it **did**.	No, it **didn't**.
Yes, they **did**.	No, they **didn't**.

WH- QUESTIONS

Wh- word	*Did*	Subject	Verb
When	**did**	the storm	**begin**?
Where	**did**	you	**stay**?
How many days	**did**	it	**rain**?
How much damage	**did**	you	**have**?

WHO QUESTIONS

Who	Verb	
Who	**helped**	their neighbors after the storm?
Who	**saw**	the tornado?

UNIT 10

HAVE TO / HAS TO

I You They	**have to**	**go** through security.
She	**has to**	**bring** photo ID.

DON'T HAVE TO / DOESN'T HAVE TO

I You We They	don't		order the invitations.
		have to	work today.
He She	doesn't		

Note:

Don't have to and *doesn't have to* are modals. They show that an action is not necessary.

Have to / Has to

YES / NO QUESTIONS

Do	I you we they		work overtime?
		have to	send a gift?
Does	he she		

ANSWERS

Yes, you **do**.	No, you **don't**.
Yes, I **do**.	No, I **don't**.
Yes, we **do**.	No, we **don't**.
Yes, they **do**.	No, they **don't**.
Yes, he **does**.	No, he **doesn't**.
Yes, she **does**.	No, she **doesn't**.

HAD TO / DIDN'T HAVE TO

I You He They	had to didn't have to	work. send a gift.

Notes:

1. *Had to* and *didn't have to* are modals.
2. *Had to* is the past of *have to* and *has to*.
3. *Didn't have to* is the past of *don't have to* and *doesn't have to*.

SHOULD / SHOULDN'T

You **should wear** your blue dress.
She **shouldn't get** married now.
She **should finish** college first.

Notes:

1. *Should* is a modal. *Should* gives advice or an opinion.
2. *Should* has the same form for all persons.

UNIT 11

CAN

I **can install** internet service in your home.
He **can change** the lights in your home.

Notes:

1. *Can* is a modal. It shows ability.
2. *Can* has the same form for all persons.

COULD YOU / WOULD YOU

Could you please call Mr. Smith?
Would you please help this customer?

Notes:

1. *Could you* and *Would you* are modals. Use these expressions to make polite requests.
2. *Could you* and *Would you* have the same form for all persons.

MUST / MUST NOT / CAN'T

I **must** wear a name tag.
We **must** sign in.
You **must not** make personal calls at work.
You **can't** use your cellphone.

Notes:

1. *Must, must not*, and *can't* are modals. They explain rules, policies, and regulations.

2. *Must* and *have to* are similar in meaning.

   I **must wear** a uniform.   I **have to wear** a uniform.

3. *Must not* and *can't* show that an action is not allowed or permitted.

4. Be careful! *Must not* and *(not) have to* do not have the same meaning.

   I **must not bring** my children to work. ≠ I **don't have to** bring my children to work.

   Must not refers to an action that is not allowed. *Don't have to* refers to something that is not necessary.

5. *Must, must not*, and *can't* have the same form for all persons.

MAY AND MIGHT

I **may** quit my job.
The company **might** close.

Notes:

1. *May* and *might* are modals. They show possibility.

2. *May* and *might* have the same form for all persons.

UNIT 12

PRESENT TIME CLAUSES

He watches TV <u>**before** he goes to bed</u>.
(main clause)   (time clause)

<u>**Before** he goes to bed</u>, he watches TV.
(time clause)   (main clause)

Notes:

1. A time clause explains when an action happens. A time clause begins with a word such as *after, before, when, as soon as, until,* or *if*. A time clause has a subject and a verb.

2. If the time clause is at the beginning of the sentence, use a comma after the time clause. If the time clause is at the end of the sentence, don't use a comma.

   When Henry gets home, he makes dinner.

   The children watch TV **until** their father comes home.

PHRASAL VERBS

Some verbs in English are made up of two words. They are called *phrasal verbs*.
   Anna likes to **get up** early on Sundays.
Some phrasal verbs can have other words between the two parts of the verb. These are called separable (S) verbs.
   I **put on** my coat.   I **put** my coat **on**.
Some phrasal verbs can't have other words between the two parts of the verb.
   I **get on** the bus at 7:30 every morning.   NOT   ~~I **get** the bus **on** at 7:30 every morning.~~

UNIT 13

I locked my door **before** I went to work.   **Before** I went to work, I locked my door.
  (main clause)   (time clause)   (time clause)   (main clause)

PAST CONTINUOUS

I	was	read**ing**.
You	were	work**ing**.
He	was	sleep**ing**.
She	was	play**ing**.
It	was	mak**ing** noise.
We	were	watch**ing** TV.
They	were	driv**ing**.

Note:

The past continuous describes an action that was in progress at a specific time in the past.

PAST CONTINUOUS WITH *WHILE*

While I **was driving** to school, I **was listening** to the radio.
I **was listening** to the radio **while** I **was driving** to school.

Note:

Use *while* with the past continuous to show that two actions were happening at the same time.

THE PAST CONTINUOUS AND THE SIMPLE PAST

I **heard** someone in my living room while I **was sleeping**.
Boris **was eating** dinner when someone **knocked** at his door.

Note:

The past continuous can describe an action that was interrupted. One action was going on when another action happened.

UNIT 14

Future Time Clauses

STATEMENTS

She **will get** a good job after she **graduates** from college.
  (main clause)   (time clause)
After she **graduates** from college, she **will get** a good job.
    (time clause)   (main clause)

Note:

The verb in the main clause is in the future (with *will* or *going to*). The verb in the time clause is in the present.

QUESTIONS

What are you going to do after you graduate?
Where is he going to live when his company transfers him?
Before he starts his new job, **is he going to take a vacation**?

Note:

In a question with a future time clause, use the future question form in the main clause.

APPENDIX B | Spelling Rules

Plural Nouns

1. For most nouns, add an -s.
   boy – boys   store – stores   student – students

2. If a noun ends with a consonant and a *y*, change the *y* to *i*, and add -es.
   city – cities   dictionary – dictionaries   baby – babies

3. If a noun ends with *sh, ch, x,* or *z*, add -es.
   box – boxes   dish – dishes   watch – watches

Present Continuous Verbs

1. For most verbs, add -ing.
   walk – walking   play – playing   eat – eating

2. If a verb ends in *e*, drop the *e* and add -ing.
   write – writing   come – coming   drive – driving

3. If a verb ends in a consonant + vowel + consonant, double the final consonant and add -ing.
   sit – sitting   run – running   put – putting

4. If a verb ends in *w, x,* or *y*, do not double the consonant. Add -ing.
   play – playing   relax – relaxing   snow – snowing

Present Verbs: Third Person

1. For most verbs, add -s.
   make – makes   call – calls   sleep – sleeps

2. If a verb ends with a consonant and a *y*, change the *y* to *i*, and add -es.
   try – tries   cry – cries   apply – applies

3. If a verb ends with *sh, ch, x,* or *z*, add -es.
   wash – washes   watch – watches   fix – fixes

4. These verbs are irregular in the third person.
   have – has   do – does

Past Verbs

1. For most verbs, add -d or -ed.
   save – saved   rent – rented

2. If a verb ends in a consonant + *y*, change the *y* to *i* and add -ed.
   try – tried   study – studied

3. If a verb ends in a consonant + vowel + consonant, double the final consonant and add -ed.
   stop – stopped   rob – robbed

4. If a verb ends in *w, x,* or *y*, do not double the consonant. Add -ed.
   play – played   relax – relaxed   snow – snowed

Comparative Adjectives: -er

1. For most adjectives, add -r or -er.
   large – larger   *short – shorter*   *tall – taller*

2. If a one-syllable adjective ends in a consonant + vowel + consonant, double the final consonant and add -er.
   big – bigger   *thin – thinner*   *sad – sadder*

3. If an adjective ends in a consonant + *y*, change the *y* to *i* and add -er.
   happy – happier   *heavy – heavier*   *friendly – friendlier*

Superlative Adjectives: -est

1. For most adjectives, add -st or -est.
   large – largest   *short – shortest*   *tall – tallest*

2. If a one-syllable adjective ends in a consonant + vowel + consonant, double the final consonant and add -est.
   big – biggest   *thin – thinnest*   *sad – saddest*

3. If an adjective ends in a consonant + *y*, change the *y* to *i* and add -est.
   busy – busiest   *noisy – noisiest*   *friendly – friendliest*

APPENDIX C Student to Student

UNIT 2

Student 1: Read the sentences in Set A to Student 2.

Student 2: Read the sentences in Set B to Student 1.

Set A
a. He gets up late.
b. He plays tennis.
c. He studies in the morning.
d. He doesn't pick up his clothes.
e. He makes his bed.
f. He gets up early.

Set B
a. He doesn't get up early.
b. He keeps his things neat.
c. He takes morning classes.
d. He studies at night.
e. He plays basketball.
f. He doesn't make his bed.

UNIT 4

Student 1: Ask your partner about Canada. Complete the chart below.

Student 2: Ask your partner about Mexico. Complete the chart on page 56.

How much tourism is there in Canada?

There is a lot of tourism in Canada.

	Mexico	Canada
Tourism	a lot	
Deserts	two	
Mountains	many	
National parks	67	
Snow	very little	
Ski resorts	one	
Official languages	one	

UNIT 6

Student 1: Read the questions in Set A to Student 2.

Student 2: Read the questions in Set B to Student 1.

Set A
1. How are you feeling?
2. Are you going to need an operation?
3. How long are you going to stay in the hospital?
4. When are you going home?
5. What other tests are you going to need?

Set B
1. What's the problem?
2. When is the doctor going to talk to you?
3. When are they going to take X-rays?
4. When are you going to know the test results?
5. When are you going to return to school?

UNIT 7

Student 1: Read the questions in Set A to Student 2.

Student 2: Read the questions in Set B to Student 1.

Set A
1. Which city is the most populated?
2. Which city has the highest percentage of Hispanics?
3. Which city has the highest median household income?
4. Which city has the least expensive houses?
5. In which city do workers have the longest commute?
6. Which city has the most rainfall?
7. Which city has the fewest sunny days?

Set B
1. Which city has the lowest population?
2. Which city has the lowest unemployment?
3. Which city has the most expensive houses?
4. In which city do workers have the shortest commute?
5. Which city has the lowest median household income?
6. Which city has the least rain?
7. Which city receives the most snow?

APPENDIX D / Dictation

UNIT 2

1. The average person wears a seat belt.
2. 10% of people don't wear a seat belt.
3. The average person lives in a house.
4. More than half of Americans own their homes.
5. Many people rent their homes.

UNIT 6

1. A man was in an accident.
2. Another driver hit his car.
3. He stayed in the hospital overnight.
4. He's going to call his insurance company today.
5. He's going to report the accident.
6. He is also going to call his lawyer.
7. He's going to sue the other driver.
8. The accident was the woman's fault.
9. She was talking on her cellphone at the time of the accident.

UNIT 7

1. India is as interesting as China.
2. India isn't as large as China.
3. India is almost as populated as China.
4. India is as diverse as China.
5. Chinese food isn't as spicy as Indian food.

UNIT 8

1. Yolanda's father had a job offer in Florida.
2. He moved his family to Tampa.
3. Yolanda and Diego liked Largo.
4. They lived there for two years.
5. After Yolanda had a baby, they moved back to Tampa.
6. Yolanda needed to go back to work.
7. Diego's job just offered him a promotion.

UNIT 12

Mimi has a difficult time falling asleep at night. She gets in bed and puts her head on the pillow. But as soon as she closes her eyes, she begins to worry—about her job, her health, and her family. So, she now has a routine to relax herself before she goes to sleep. Before she goes into her bedroom, she drinks a cup of hot herbal tea. Then, she brushes her teeth. After she brushes her teeth, she washes her face and puts on her favorite face cream. When she gets into bed, she picks up a magazine and reads for a few minutes. Then, she listens to some quiet music. When she finally turns off her light, she falls asleep more easily.

UNIT 14

1. Maria is going to look for a job before she graduates.
2. Before she looks for a job, she will write her resume.
3. She will send out her resume when she sees a good job posting.
4. If she hears of a job opening, she will call the company.
5. When she goes on an interview, she is going to wear a suit.
6. If she makes a good impression, the company will hire her.

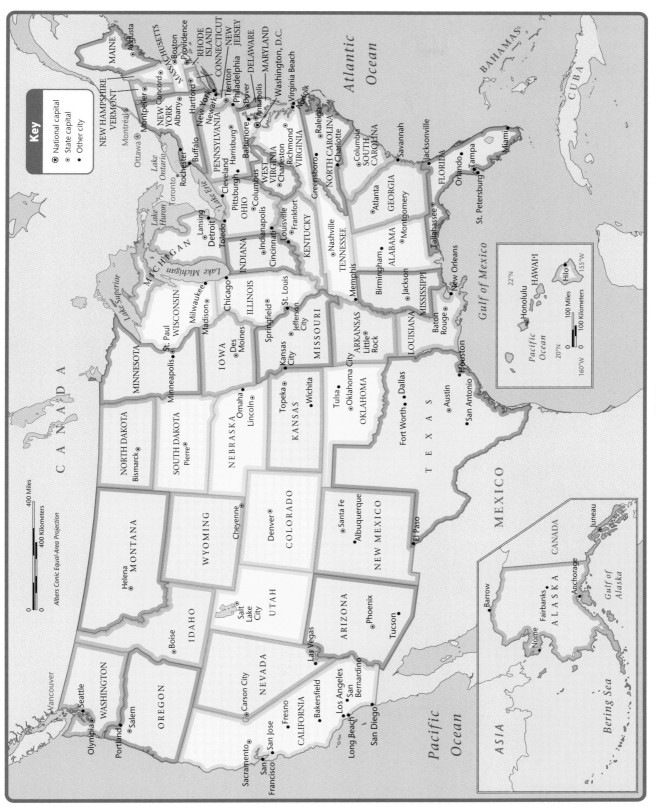

US Map

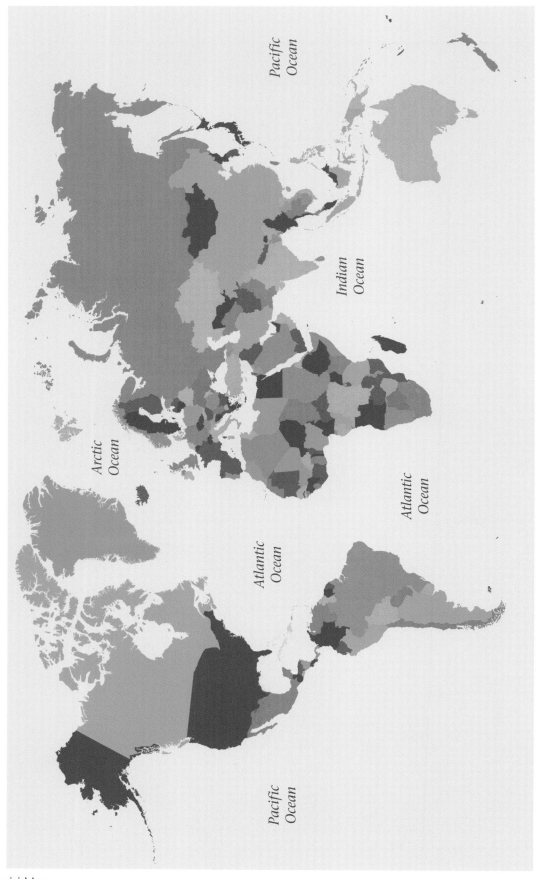

World Map

iv (left) Dick Loek/Getty Images, **iv** (left) Tony Shi Photography/Getty Images, **iv** (left) KAZUHIRO NOGI/Getty Images, **iv** (left) Paul Horsted/Stock Connection/Aurora Photos, **iv** (left) Keystone-France/Getty Images, **iv** (left) Matt Cardy/Getty Images, **iv** (left) Woods Wheatcroft/Aurora Photos, **iv** (left) ©Wolfe House Movers, LLC, **vi** (left) ROBIN UTRECHT/Getty Images, **vi** (left) Jeff Kolodny Photography, **vi** (left) Mike Harrington/Getty Images, **vi** (left) FREDERICK FLORIN/Getty Images, **vi** (left) Lorado/Getty Images, **vi** (left) Caren Brinkema/Getty Images, **2** (left) Siri Stafford/Getty Images, **4** (bottom left) Jetta Productions/Getty Images, **5** (bottom left) Steve Debenport/Getty Images, **5** (bottom right) Jordi Angrill/Getty Images, **10** (bottom) Rawpixel.com/Shutterstock.com, **12** (bottom center) witsanu deetuam/Shutterstock.com, **14** (center right) John Coletti/Getty Images, **17** (center) Tony Shi Photography/Getty Images, **18** (top center) Boston Globe/Getty Images, **28** (bottom center) ©Ken Wolter/Shutterstock, **30** (top center) WIN-Initiative/Getty Images, **33** (center) KAZUHIRO NOGI/Getty Images, **34** (top) Erik Isakson/Getty Images, **36** (top) Phanie/Alamy Stock Photo Stock Photo, **37** (top right) jsmith/Getty Images, **44** (bottom) J. Emilio Flores/The New York Times, **46** (bottom) MirageC/Getty Images, **49** (center) Paul Horsted/Stock Connection/Aurora Photos, **50** (top) Raico Rosenberg/AGE Fotostock, **51** (top right) Clarence Holmes Photography/Alamy Stock Photo, **58** (top) Mike Criss/National Geographic My Shot/National Geographic Creative, **60-61** (top) stevemendenhall/Getty Images, **62** (top) amadeustx/Shutterstock.com, **65** (center) Keystone-France/Getty Images, **66** (top left) Scanrail1/Shutterstock.com, **66** (top center) bfk/Shutterstock.com, **66** (top right) mustafagull/Getty Images, **66** (top left) T3 Magazine/Getty Images, **66** (top left) Howard Kingsnorth/Getty Images, **66** (bottom right) Gargantiopa/Shutterstock.com, **69** (center left) Lyn Alweis/Getty Images, **69** (top left) Andrey_Popov/Shutterstock.com, **71** (top center) Tooga/Getty Images, **71** (top) fizkes/Shutterstock.com, **71** (top) Caroline von Tuempling/Getty Images, **71** (bottom right) Steve Debenport/Getty Images, **74** (top left) PhotoAlto/Odilon Dimier/Getty Images, **74** (top left) Ed Norton/Getty Images, **74** (top center) Jordan Siemens/Getty Images, **74** (center left) quavondo/ E+/Getty Images, **81** (center) Matt Cardy/Getty Images, **82** (top) Portland Press Herald/Getty Images, **82** (top) Joe Raedle/Getty Images, **82** (top) Cultura Creative (RF)/Alamy Stock Photo, **82** (center) Wavebreak Media ltd/Alamy Stock Photo, **84** (top) tab62/Shutterstock.com, **86** (bottom center) Sam Mellish/Getty Images, **87** (bottom) Art Directors & TRIP/Alamy Stock Photo, **92** (center) Melissa Farlow/Aurora Photos, **96** (top right) Don Bartletti/Getty Images, **97** (center) Woods Wheatcroft/Aurora Photos, **98** (top left) maximkabb/Getty Images, **98** (top left) Ian G Dagnall/Alamy Stock Photo, **98** (top left) Andrew Peacock/Aurora Photos, **98** (top left) Alexey Rotanov/Shutterstock.com, **98** (top left) Twin Design/Shutterstock.com, **98** (top left) ZUMA Press, Inc./Alamy Stock Photo, **104** (bottom left) Xiaolu Chu/Getty Images, **104** (bottom right) Soltan Frédéric/Getty Images, **106** (top right) logoboom/Shutterstock.com, **106** (bottom) Eduard Moldoveanu/500px, **107** (bottom center) Paul Giamou/Getty Images, **108** (bottom center) David McNew/Getty Images, **110** (bottom left) Stefano Ravera/Alamy Stock Photo, **112** (bottom center) Planet Observer/UIG/Getty Images, **113** (center) ©Wolfe House Movers, LLC, **114** (top center) Rob Crandall/Shutterstock.com, **115** (bottom center) Klaus Tiedge/Getty Images, **117** (bottom center) Blaine Harrington III/Alamy Stock Photo, **124** (bottom center) Baltimore Sun/Getty Images, **129** (center) ROBIN UTRECHT/Getty Images, **130** (center left) Peter J. Wilson/Shutterstock.com, **130** (center) David Dreambular/Shutterstock.com, **130** (center left) MDay Photography/Shutterstock.com, **130** (center) Cultura RM/Alamy Stock Photo, **130** (bottom) Theo Allofs/Getty Images, **130** (bottom) hepatus/Getty Images, **130** (bottom) eddtoro/Shutterstock.com, **130** (center) Blend Images - REB Images/Getty Images, **130** (center) Tom Wang/Shutterstock.com, **131** (bottom center) Ray Bulson/Getty Images, **134** (bottom) US Army Photo / Alamy Stock Photo, **134** (bottom) macknimal/Shutterstock.com, **136** (bottom) Josh Reynolds/apimages.com, **140** (bottom) Cultura Creative (RF)/Alamy Stock Photo, **142** (bottom) Kevin Horan/Getty Images, **143** (bottom) Ho New/Reuters, **145** (top) Jeff Kolodny Photography, **147** (bottom) Sean Pavone/Shutterstock.com, **151** (bottom) trekandshoot/Shutterstock.com, **154** (center right) STAN HONDA/Getty Images, **156** (top) John Henley/Getty Images, **158** (top) Dua Aftab / EyeEm/Getty Images, **160** (center) Eugenio Marongiu/Shutterstock.com, **160** (center) Studio Intra/Shutterstock.com, **160** (top) Minerva Studio/Shutterstock.com, **160** (center) Olyver Whyte/Shutterstock.com, **161** (center) Mike Harrington/Getty Images, **162** (top center) Reza Estakhrian/Getty Images, **162** (top) Pressmaster/Shutterstock.com, **162** (top) 2p2play/Shutterstock.com, **162** (top left) Mint Images Limited/Alamy Stock Photo, **165** (bottom center) Juan Napurí/Alamy Stock Photo, **172** (bottom) g-stockstudio/Getty Images, **174** (center) Jeff Greenberg/Getty Images, **177** (center) FREDERICK FLORIN/Getty Images, **179** (bottom right) Ariel Skelley/Getty Images, **183** (bottom) Maximilian Stock Ltd./Getty Images, **186** (bottom) Tim Hursley, **191** (center) Lorado/Getty Images, **192** (center) SpeedKingz/Shutterstock.com, **192** (top center) Westend61/Getty Images, **192** (center) Christian Delbert/Shutterstock.com, **192** (center) Adam Gault/Getty Images, **197** (bottom) South_agency/Getty Images, **198** (bottom) Thomas Trutschel/Getty Images, **198** (bottom) Chase Jarvis/Getty Images, **198** (bottom) LightField Studios/Shutterstock.com, **198** (bottom) Mike Focus/Shutterstock.com, **202** (bottom) PNC/Getty Images, **205** (center) Caren Brinkema/Getty Images, **206** (top) Macrovector/Shutterstock.com, **208** (center left) Andrey_Popov/Shutterstock.com, **208** (center) g-stockstudio/Shutterstock.com, **208** (center left) Hero Images/Getty Images, **208** (center) Blend Images - Hill Street Studios/Getty Images, **208** (center) David R. Frazier Photolibrary, Inc./Alamy Stock Photo, **208** (top) anyaivanova/Shutterstock.com, **212** (bottom) Steve Weinrebe/Getty Images, **213** (bottom right) PG Arphexad/Alamy Stock Photo, **216** (bottom left) Agencja Fotograficzna Caro/Alamy Stock Photo Stock Photo, **217** Alex Hinds/Shutterstock.com, **218** (bottom) Spencer Rowell/Getty Images, **241** seeyah panwan/Shutterstock.com, **242** National Geographic Maps

All illustrations Cengage Learning.